PERMANENT FIRES:
Reviews of Poetry, 1958-1973

by

RAY SMITH

with a Preface by
Ervin J. Gaines

The Scarecrow Press, Inc.
Metuchen, N.J.   1975

Library of Congress Cataloging in Publication Data

Smith, Ray, 1915-
   Permanent fires.

   Bibliography: p.
   Includes index.
   1. Poetry--Book reviews. I. Title.
PN1136.S58   821'.009   74-22230
ISBN 0-8108-0757-2

For
Thomas P. Beyer,
teacher and friend

CONTENTS

PREFACE

To give weight to Shelley's grand pronouncement that "poets are the unacknowledged legislators of the world," our century has given us Neruda, Paz, Pasternak, and many lesser spirits whose voices haunt our dreams, whose light leads us in mysterious ways through the caves of our social torment. The power of poetry in our century has not been diluted, even though it is little in evidence in the market-places of our times.

Ray Smith is an extraordinary man. Himself a poet, he knows, better than most, that the wise words of the visionary men and women we call poets are the elixir of life. He calls us to our duty to heed the distant voices. For many years now Smith has reminded librarians of the care they must exercise to give place on their shelves to the often slight and fragile volumes of poetry that almost disappear in the tumult.

He has gladly and with great dedication taken upon himself the obligation of tacking up on the world's bulletin boards the announcements that wisdom by Berryman, Ransom, Sachs, or Shapiro is available.

His many reviews in popular publications have brought important works to the attention of the man in the street and to the libraries of the nation. His services are invaluable. There are too few of us who care as deeply and as passionately about poetry as Ray Smith. We are all in his debt.

vii

This volume gathers in one place his ephemeral reviews, which might otherwise have been lost. Together they give us a perspective about Smith but, more important, about the state of poetry in the world.

Ervin J. Gaines
Director
Minneapolis Public Library

INTRODUCTION

Poetry is durable speech, or to adapt a metaphor from a book reviewed here (and taken from Raleigh), durable or "permanent fires. " Unlike headlines, poems are always timely and not so often shouldered aside by newtitleism as most publication.

In their range these books reviewed across a fifteen-year span may offer a sampler like the mood census taken by a Chinese emperor who collected his people's poems in order to read their state of mind. Our platform confessional verse anticipated group therapy. Ted Hughes and Alan Sillitoe tell more in spare crisis-laden work than can be gathered anywhere else within comparable compass about their England. And the late Ramon Guthrie's "christoi"-- his personal heroes of resistance and art--can herald a hopeful emergent phase beyond such trends.

Included are 131 reviews and annotations from 1958 through 1973, selected from more than 200 considered. They appeared in Library Journal and later the Minneapolis Sunday Tribune and (daily) Star. They introduced The Sixties--now The Seventies--Press of Robert Bly, which emphasized less familiar "non-British traditions" through Vallejo, Trakl and others who are now part of our poetic consciousness.

Gunnar Ekelof of Sweden, Wole Soyinka of Nigeria, Nelly Sachs of Germany, are reviewed, along with collected or selected work by Eliot, Ransom, Deutsch, MacDiarmid, Cowley; and a range in time from Villon to Levertov (though the weight is heavily modern), in setting from the bucolic Georgian Ralph Hodgson to the urban tough Charles Bukowski. There are Stevens, Berryman, Lowell, among the best known; the unaccountably too-little-known Edwin Honig; and some known regionally or little at all. I reached back to 1948, when I had been doing reviews for Poetry, to retrieve one published a quarter-century before my latest review of the same writer, May Sarton.

Arrangement is alphabetical by author (or in a few instances by subject). Library Journal and Poetry pieces. are identified; the others, almost always longer, are from the Minneapolis Tribune and Star.

During review and speaking activity for poetry in libraries I chastised the Notable Books Council (ALA) for including few or no books of poetry in its lists of the early '60s, and was suitably rewarded by service on that body (1964-67); I feel obliged to point to some backsliding by the Council. Touching the personal note again, I recall with pleasure the Iowa Library Association conference at Sioux City in 1964, the year of my presidency; its theme, "A Festival of Imagination." The main speaker, the late Henry Rago, editor of Poetry, mainly read and then re-read short poems by Yeats to show that poetry is speech--permanent speech--to a gratifying reception.

During the dozen years of reviewing for Library Journal I was only once engaged in controversy by a publisher--who thought one of his authors had been scanted in an omnibus review. Kind responses came from John Martin, editor of the Black Sparrow Press, from the Blys of the Sixties Press, and others. A pleasant correspondence opened with elder poet Ramon Guthrie when he wrote a courteous note to correct a blunder in my review of his <u>Maximum Security Ward</u>. Once I asked him to tell more about a meeting with Hemingway in Paris at Robert Desnos's during the Spanish Civil War, concerned with getting ambulances to the Spanish Loyalists. I quote his reply--short, exact, and holding some of the interest of his poems which combine his own history with social causes:

> There's not much to tell about me and Hemingway's ambulances.
> We were at Desnos's for dinner and he asked me to go to Le Havre when they came in and take them to Madrid. I consented. He told me to keep in touch with him: he would tell me when they arrived. I did and he didn't.
> I think that he had already arranged with Evan Shipman to take them. Shipman got as far as Toulouse with them, lingered in bars there and got arrested and expelled--to Spain. I don't know what became of the ambulances. Maybe he took them with him.
> I heard that he acquitted himself very well in Spain, but no word of the ambulances.

Special mention must be made of Pablo Neruda. Not reviewed here, his poetry should be a first choice in every library, public and personal--and first of all, <u>The Heights of Macchu Picchu.</u> His death in September 1973 was probably hastened by the violent overthrow of the Allende government in his native Chile. Neruda symbolizes the poet "involved in mankind."

Every review, however short, ought to introduce book and author, describe or intimate the book's distinctive character or flavor, and place or evaluate it. The new book by a well-known poet can be compared with his previous work. That of one less well known will need more attention to affinities, personal manner, themes. Reviews--annotations especially--should aim for concision, concrete word or telling quotation, coherence, emphasis on major point or theme, suggestive start and earned conclusion. The reviewer's judgment should come when, after reading and rereading, he emerges from experiencing the poetry to reattain critical "distance."

Courses in library book selection benefit by including analysis of the short review such as the Library Journal annotation: its effectiveness overall, structurally, sentence by sentence, even word by word. Economy, involved in concision, does not always mean the fewest words; it does mean precise and appropriate words. Book interpretation should be bracketed with book selection as a professional function.

Acknowledgments are made to R. R. Bowker (Library Journal), Poetry, and the Minneapolis Star and Tribune, for permissions to reprint. I owe a debt to the late John K. Sherman, formerly in charge of the Minneapolis books and arts pages; it was he who first called and asked me to review, and when he relinquished the Tribune for the Star alone I did likewise as a reviewer. Subsequently he sweetened the first months of my three years on the West coast by continuing to send books after me, always subject to my own decision whether or not to review, which removed pressure. Those who knew him or about him will recall his long service to all the arts. The index, much assistance and the idea for the whole thing I owe to my wife, Mara (a university bibliographer). I also wish to thank Eric Moon, editor of Library Journal during most of my reviewing association with it, for his many services on behalf of poetry in libraries; Lawrence Clark Powell for writing Books in My Baggage; and Ervin J. Gaines, Director of the Minneapolis Public Library and a fine reviewer, whose unfailing courtesy to other librarians gave this book its preface.

Ray Smith

REVIEWS OF POETRY

DONALD M. ALLEN (editor)

The New American Poetry: 1945-1960. Grove, 1960, 454 pages.

From small presses, broadsheets and magazines this anthology gathered 215 poems by 44 poets on the "beat" line in five groups of whom the "Beats proper" (Ginsberg, Kerouac) and the San Francisco poets led by Ferlinghetti are best known. Among others: Robert Duncan, Gregory Corso, Robert Creeley, and Denise Levertov (with a fine selection). Ginsberg's "Howl," extravagantly called "The Waste Land of our age" by Allen, stands as manifesto. In the closing prose section Charles Olson's "Projective Verse" emphasizes their technical ancestry in W. C. Williams and Pound and calls for open ("field") composition, and relative in place of metrical measure. Of general interest, but many poems are exhibitionist or suggest runaway typewriters, and a new jargon has emerged to counterbalance the jargon of the academics. LJ

JOHN ASHBERY

Three Poems. Viking, 1972, 118 pages.

The frequently long paragraphs of John Ashbery's

1

<u>Three Poems</u>, sometimes several pages in length, are
adapted to on-running reverie. Insistently abstract, Ashbery's book requires undeviating attention from the reader,
who may balk at its digressions, its "stops and starts of
the mind," and the attenuated elegance of Ashbery's diction.

"The motion of the story is moving though not getting
nearer," Ashbery writes in his introspective trilogy, the sections of which are entitled "The New Spirit," "The System"
and "The Recital." Yet Ashbery perseveres in trying to
landscape the withinness of experience under temporal flow
and change, and endeavors to be "ruled by these strings or
emanations that connect everything together."

Among his themes are the relativity of awareness,
loss and renewal in the self ("we are rescued by what we
cannot imagine"), a new identity accrued from many selves,
and the role and difficulty and necessity of choice. The
reader follows a tenuous argument around Ashbery's labyrinth,
exhorted now and then by the poet: "What do you think to
gain by merely standing there looking worried...?"

The author of six previous volumes of poetry, most
recently <u>The Double Dream of Spring</u>, Ashbery is identified
with the New York School of poets along with Kenneth Koch,
Barbara Guest and Frank O'Hara. He shares their devo-
tion to verbal gamesmanship and literary elitism. Now
executive editor of <u>Art News,</u> he lived for nearly a decade
in Paris (1955-65) on a Fulbright grant and as an art
columnist.

<u>Three Poems</u> is cerebral, sophisticated, cinematic,
thin, fatiguing and "continually straying over the border into
the positive past and the negative future." For those readers who can and will cope with his vagueness and complexity,

John Ashbery's book offers his own particular thing, poems
of sensibility in a new key.

W. H. AUDEN

Homage to Clio.   Random House, 1960, 91 pages.

      In prose "Interlude" notations about love and poems,
midway in his book, Auden says he first demands of others'
poetry "that it be good," of his own that it be "recogniz-
able ... as having been written, for better or worse, by
me." The mature Auden signature is here, virtuosity of a
high order, instruction set to music, clarity, measure, and
wit ("What reverence is rightly paid/ To a Divinity so odd/
He lets the Adam whom He made/ Perform the Acts of
God?").   Auden has taught the Muse manners--and insistent
mannerisms--until his modern Augustan style and tone seem
while we read the most authentic of poetic performances.
To Clio, the muse responsible for history, he addresses his
volume; separating her domain from that of Aphrodite and
Artemis (who rule non-human nature), "Major Powers" that
"Can be represented in granite," he domesticates Clio too:
"what icon/ Have the arts for you, who look like any/
Girl one has not noticed...." True, what he says in more
memorable speech has often been said before.   "The History
of Science" tells us "That one can err his way to riches, /
Win glory by mistake...." "The Old Man's Road" (religion)
belongs "to those/ Who love it no less since it lost purpose,... / Assuming a freedom its Powers deny, / Denying
its Powers, they pass freely."   A large proportion of light
verse, an Auden specialty, includes limericks and a final
section of "Academic Graffiti."   LJ

MARGARET AVISON

The Dumbfounding. Norton, 1966, 99 pages.

    These sacramental imagist poems are luminous with
wonder. The title poem "The Dumbfounding," "A Story,"
"The Word" and others are Christian both in reference and
inspiration. But through them all, terse and musical, shines
a palpable reverence for life. "Unspeakable" concerns "The
beauty of the unused," "A Nameless One" the brief life-
span of an insect. In "Thaw" Sunday-dressed children stare
as "Limewater and licorice light/ wander the tumbled
streets." Percipient, transforming the average day, these
poems achieve (or reveal) moments bathed in a consummate
vision.   LJ

WENDELL BERRY

Openings. Harcourt, Brace & World, 1968, 67 pages.

    These are poems of direct statement and concise
description, quiet and nearly always in short free forms.
They combine nature and what man has brought into nature:

> ... engines marking the country
> like an audible map, the high dark
> marked by the flight of men,
> lights stranger than stars.
> The phoebes cross and re-cross
> the openings, alert
> for what may still be earned
> from the light.

    Berry, "teacher, farmer, and writer," is on the
English faculty at the University of Kentucky and has published two novels as well as an earlier collection of poems,

The Broken Ground (1964).   The Kentucky countryside, its
seasons and creatures and appearances, are at the book's
core and interfuse it all.

But the celebration of nature is matched by social
concerns.   The sense of danger from the world outside the
writer's Kentucky retreat comes in a number of poems, among
them "To My Children Fearing for Them":

> Terrors are to come.   The earth
> is poisoned with narrow lives.
> I think of you.   What you will
> live through, or perish by, eats
> at my heart.

The poet suggests a partial answer in "To a Siberian
Woodsman, " a song of international comradeship written in
Whitmanic rhythms: "Who has invented our enmity?   Who
has prescribed us hatred of each other?   Who has armed us
against each other with the death of the world?"

The book's long poem, "Window Poems, " is not sustained throughout and grows wordy and slack.   As it does
very infrequently outside the longer effort, moralizing edges
out the lyrical:

> And now his mighty government
> wants to help everybody
> even if it has to kill them
> to do it--like the fellow in the story
> who helped his neighbor to Heaven....

Berry does most as a poet when he transcribes, with
a minimum of extension, the natural setting from which he
and his reader can take renewal:

> Now after the evening storm
> the wind blows fresh off the hills,
> the ripples speed against
> the current, the air clears,
> a kingfisher turns
> the rusty hinges of his song.

JOHN BERRYMAN

His Toy, His Dream, His Rest.   Farrar, Straus & Giroux,
1968, 317 pages.

These poems, in motion from the opening "posthu-
mous" ones to the stunning next to last at the suicide father's
grave, can't be contained and will hardly go away.   In the
last, Henry--the speaker in the poems--turns from the un-
tenable lightness of the "mouldering grave clothes" to "my
heavy daughter. "

Berryman's toy is a compressed, freely rhymed six-
line stanza, language and syntax free style, three to a song.
From "Op. posth. no. 4":

> But this is death--
> which in some vain strive many to avoid,
> many.   It's on its way, where you drop at
> who stood up.   Scrunch down small.
>
> It wasn't so much after all to lose, was, Boyd?
> A body. --But, Mr. Bones, you needed that.
> Now I put on my tall hat.

77 Dream Songs (1964), which these 308 additions continue and conclude, brought in Henry as a device permitting
the poet to talk with himself in any person desired, sometimes joined by the unnamed second speaker who calls Henry
"Mr. Bones. "   The latter comes infrequently into this new
dialogue of self and soul, a log of doings and happenings over
eleven years of composition, overshadowed by spiritual
weather and "an irreversible loss. "

Vietnam, LBJ, the Soviet trial of the poet Joseph
Brodsky, are among public events alluded to.   Mostly Henry,
happy because of the author's prefatory disclaimer, does what
Berryman does, revisits Ireland, goes to the hospital, meets
his classes, mourns the deaths of Delmore Schwartz and

Randall Jarrell, speculates about undertaking and fame:

> having much to say, masterless after all, & gay
> with probability; time being on his side,
> the large work largely done,
> over the years, the prizes mostly won,
> we work now for ourself alone, away
> from even pal & wife, in ways not to be denied.

Obsessed as they are intense, the songs are heavy on Henry's "Large work, which will appear--and baffle everybody. " And sitting over there in Ireland, "Adorable country," Henry wouldn't let sit in on his combo the whole of Iowa, "Detestable state, made of swine and corn/ rich and ignorant, pastless, with one great tree in it. "

"After thirty falls I rush back to the haunts of Yeats," Henry writes. "I have moved to Dublin to have it out with you, / majestic Shade. " Which just can't help but recall Berryman's line on Frost in the "Dream Songs": "While he begins to have it out with Horace. "

The dream may after all have presented Henry as a candidate to write all over one of the four walls in the new Jerusalem. It's hard to get past the terrifying, splendid song no. 384.

> The marker slants, flowerless, day's almost done,
> I stand above my father's grave with rage,...
> who shot his heart out in a Florida dawn
> O ho alas alas
> When will indifference come, I moan & rave
> I'd like to scrabble till I get right down
> away down under the grass
> to axe the casket open ha to see
> just how he's taking it, which he sought so hard.

JOHN BERRYMAN

77 Dream Songs.   Farrar, 1964, 84 pages.

"Let's be quiet. Let us listen:/ --What for, Mr.
Bones?/ --while he begins to have it out with Horace. "
These lines from the last of several poems about Frost ex-
emplify Berryman's dialogue form, with Henry and Mr. Bones
alternating. The free-rhyming, six-line stanzas, with dream-
association movement, colloquial, elliptical, hark back to the
octaves of Homage to Mistress Bradstreet. Here the stanzas
are more relaxed, often neatly arrested as in "A Strut for
Roethke": "Weeds, too, he favored as most men don't
favour men. / The Garden Master's gone. " A current of
social criticism is signaled by one of the epigraphs: "Go in,
brack man, de day's yo' own. " Fractured juxtapositions and
remodeled verbs are touched by Cummings, as Berryman
ranges through the blues, satire, current events ("A Bud-
dhist, doused in the street, serenely burned"), private meditation, with sardonic quip or singing shorthand. Notable for
recreating poetry so that it enters, as poetry, into contemporary discourse.   LJ

WOLF BIERMANN

The Wire Harp: Ballads, Poems, Songs, with Musical
Scores; translated by Eric Bentley. Harcourt, Brace &
World, 1968, 98 pages.

     Wolf Biermann, alive in East Germany at this publi-
cation, was forbidden to travel, to accompany his ballads
with guitar in public, or to record his lyrics. The Wire
Harp, published in West Germany in 1965, has been translated by Eric Bentley, responsible also in large part for the
American awareness of Brecht--a writer whom Biermann
admires and resembles.

Biermann's irreverent, free, bawdy lyrics inevitably and purposefully recall Villon, the subject of a ballad in which his ghost strolls the Berlin Wall by night:

> Then for a joke he makes a harp
> Out of the Wall's barbed wire
> The guards accompany the tune
> And keep time while they fire.

Not socialist ideals but their East German malpractitioners are the targets in such polemical songs as "Do Not Wait for Better Times":

> I hear many men complaining:
> I'm a Socialist, God knows,
> But what they are fabricating
> Is the wrong suit of clothes.

Besides pleas to his fellow citizens for political criticism and change, Biermann writes against Spanish fascist oppression, and against American racism, the latter in "The Ballad of the Letter Carrier William L. Moore of Baltimore who walked alone into the Southern States in 1963. He protested against the persecution of the Negroes. He was shot after one week":

> Sunday, a blue blue day, and he
> Lay in the grass so green
> Three red carnations, crimson as blood,
> On his pale forehead were seen.

Some lyrics are wholly given over to love and wine, almost always with sardonic seasoning. Some have been fitted to the author's own musical scores by translator Bentley.

The East German official press calls Biermann a "political pornographer." It has cause for taking counsel of its fears of this unchoked voice in its midst and symbolic revival of the free-wandering Villon. The Wire Harp chalked up 40,000 sales, and this reception led to a new law prohibiting East German writers from publishing in the West without

first having submitted their work to East German publishers
and censorship.

"I will persist in truth/ I the liar," says Biermann,
himself a symbol now to German young people, impenitent,
asserting his confidence in coming times, but open-eyed:

> Berlin, I'm coolly courting you
> You're blond if not bewitching
> Your sky's a rather bitchy blue
> To it my lyre I'm hitching.

BLACK AFRICAN POETRY

Poems from Black Africa, edited with introduction by Langston Hughes.   Indiana University Press, 1963, 158 pages.

"Perhaps it is more profitable to know how people
feel than it is to know what they think," says editor Langston
Hughes.   Poems from Black Africa contains "Oral Tradi-
tionals," "English-Speaking Poets," "A Portuguese-Speaking
Poet," "French-Speaking Poets," all affirming "negritude"
--a "French-speaking" word for pride in the heritage of black
Africa.   The oral poems or songs may have local allusions;
in many tongues, as in Chinese, meaning may depend upon
tone and pitch, compounding the problem of written translation.   European educations for some African intellectuals,
and BBC-beamed programs (for which some poets have
written) account for a high proportion of stylistic modernism.

Explicit rebellion sounds in "You Tell Me To Sit
Quiet" by Jordan of South Africa, and pan-Africanism in
"Dawn in the Heart of Africa" by Lumumba, assassinated
first premier of the Congo.   More telling are simple chants
with their intimations and closeups.   Senghor, Sorbonne-edu-
cated poet of French-speaking Africa, brings a flavor of them

in "Night of Sine": "Let me listen in the smoky hut for the
shadowy visit of propitious souls, / My head on your breast
glows like a kuskus ball smoking out of the fire...." Between the derivative and the oral-native, West African Aig-
Imoukhuede's pidgin-English "One Wife for One Man" is translated line for line; example: "Bo, dis culture no waya o!"
("Man, this 'new culture' is awful").

With its informative notes this volume is an overdue
contribution (beyond many current histories and reports) to
our awareness of the complex truth presented in Nicol's
"The Meaning of Africa": "You are not a Country, Africa, /
You are a concept. "   LJ

ROBERT BLY

The Light Around the Body.   Harper & Row, 1967, 62 pages.

In The Light Around the Body, we can hear a voice
speaking from the inward life with acute and sometimes pain-
ful clarity.   Robert Bly quotes Jacob Boehme at the beginning
of a section of poems called "In Praise of Grief":

"O dear children, look in what a dungeon we are
lying, in what lodging we are; for we have been captured by
the spirit of the outward world ... it rules in our marrow
and bones. "

Immanent imagination lights up a man "moving toward
his own life, " capable, in that process, of transforming our
outward state.   Bly writes:

I have risen to a body
Not yet born,
Existing like a light around the body....

Bly has been influenced by Latin-American and

European poets writing outside the English tradition, who
turned to the inward life for imagery--such poets as Neruda,
Vallejo, and Trakl, whom he has translated and published in
his magazine The Sixties (now The Seventies, Odin House,
Madison, Minnesota).

Rejecting the dicta of the academic poet-critics who
asserted that poetry can't be written about war and politics,
Bly's writing represents and restores to poetry the wholeness
of experience.

The section "The Vietnam War" makes a compelling
protest, but does so like a spiritual seismograph registering
the shock waves in the soul:

> Let's count the bodies over again.
> If we could only make the bodies smaller,
>   The size of skulls,
> We could make a whole plain white with skulls
>   in the moonlight!
> If we could only make the bodies smaller,
>   Maybe we could get
> A whole year's kill in front of us on a desk!

Their titles give the poems' occasions; for example,
the explicit "Hatred of Men with Black Hair, " a poem ending
on lines of wonderfully poignant precision: "Underneath all
the cement of the Pentagon/ There is a drop of Indian blood
preserved in snow.... " Among other titles are "The Great
Society, " "Suddenly Turning Away, " "Moving Inward at
Last, " and "Listening to President Kennedy Lie About the
Cuban Invasion, " which I quote in entirety:

> There is another darkness,
> A darkness in the fences of the body,
> And in moles running, and telephone wires,
> And the frail ankles of horses;
> Darkness of dying grass, and yellow willow leaves;
> There is the death of broken buttonholes,
> Of brutality in high places,
> Of lying reporters.
> There is a bitter fatigue, adult and sad.

The reader finds himself forced to take an unaccus-
tomed look, perhaps at a relationship he hadn't perceived.
There is a final hallucinatory rightness in images drawn up
in their association from the unconscious:

> Light is around the petals, and behind them:
> Some petals are living on the other side of the light.
> Like sunlight drifting on to the carpet
> Where the casket stands, not knowing which world
> it is in.

This is that rarely beautiful book which ought to be
heard complete, not excerpted in a review. Intense, original, and uncomfortably relevant, it should be bought and read.

ROBERT BLY

Silence in the Snowy Fields. Wesleyan University Press,
1962, 60 pages.

The epigraph from Jacob Boehme, "We are all asleep
in the outward man, " indicates the poet's vision in his first
volume, in inward relocation of the senses: "And our skin
shall see far off, as it does under water" ("Surprised by
Evening"). In phrase rhythms, American life--a midwest
farm or a daily concern--is caught in vivid stillness, as in
"Old Boards" or "Fall": "The dusk has come, a glow in the
west, as if seen through the isinglass on old coal stoves.... "
Separate perceptions become gestures of sympathetic recognition: "And now the little houses of the grass are growing
dark" ("Snowfall in the Afternoon"). An authentically humane
and readable poetry, this has the beauty of precision within
its outwardly casual forms.   LJ

CHARLES BUKOWSKI

At Terror Street and Agony Way.   Black Sparrow Press,
1968,   89 pages.

        Bukowski probably will always write like a man driv-
ing nails into living wood and to get it out of his system.
He doesn't always drive straight or care to, as a veteran
poet of the disestablishment.   But there have crept into his
itinerant hand-to-bottle chronicle such notes as this: "The
time comes to go deeper/ into self and the time comes/
when it is more innocent/ or easier to die. " He writes
from the heartsick city, "275 steps from Hollywood, " among
"old men rolling cigarettes in rooms small enough to recog-
nize a single shadow, " "X-pugs, " Mexican cleaning girls;
or after an "automobile accident on the San Berdo freeway.
Some drunk jumped the divider.   I was the drunk. / how old
are you, daddy?/ old enough to slice the melon, I said,
tapping my cigar ashes into my beer to give me strength. "
The attractive paperbound, designed by Graham Mackintosh
for Black Sparrow Press, belongs in any library that cares
what's happening.   LJ

WITTER BYNNER

New Poems 1960.   Knopf, 1960, 134 pages.

        Witter Bynner, among the deans of our poetry, was
79 at this publication.   Since co-authoring the "Spectra" hoax
in 1916 he had had a major interest in the Orient and collab-
orated with Kiang Kang-Hu on The Jade Mountain (1929).
These brief poems seem to reflect that interest.   Aphoristic,
unified by single notions, some are instant parables, and

nearly all turn on paradox: "under a light/ he hid his
bushel. " There is much wave, water and fishing imagery:
"But the sun is still there/ Aged fisherman/ And you sit in
it fishing for people/ And hooking the sun. " With such feli-
cities, odd angles of vision and dream dislocations contribute
to an off-word idiom in poems that are tenuous, in sum, as
the old poet baits us with his sentiments and presentiments. LJ

MELVILLE CANE

Bullet-Hunting and Other New Poems.   Harcourt, 1960, 48
pages.

        "Now, in my eighth decade, no wiser now/ Than the
spellbound child" says Melville Cane in his sixth book of
verse.   But this light verse has some admonitory overtones.
"Natural History Notes" Nash-es its teeth: "The cobra/ Is
more vicious than the zebra, / Especially under Libra, / And
all through Octobra. " From this playfulness we can turn to
an Emersonian touch and intention in "Sun and Cloud, " and
to a Frostian flavor in "The Woodchuck, " expanded in the
colloquial title poem "Bullet-Hunting, a Virginia Tale. " Its
narrator describes sifting for relics on a Civil War battle-
field.   This, the longest, seems less successful than the
shorter pieces, too downright prosy, with shifts in tone and
without controlling rhythm.   The last line says, anent string-
ing bullet pellets into chains for sale to tourists, "Do you
know any better use for bullets?"   Enjoyable reading.   LJ

NANCY CARDOZO

Helmet of the Wind. Bobbs-Merrill, 1972, 86 pages.

A dozen of the poems collected in Nancy Cardozo's
Helmet of the Wind were first published in Harper's Bazaar,
The Atlantic, The New Yorker and Mademoiselle.

Her poems are spare, musical and delicate. They
try to fix the elusive and momentary in descriptions abstract
sometimes even to bodilessness ("You stand in the doorway, /
Your face is troubled. / Snow troubles the air"). Fine-
grained and crystal-like though it is, the verse can sustain
such a continuum of sensation as that recorded in "Motor-
cycling on Mt. Monadnock":

> Balanced on light we soared; the road
> Rose from its bed, but the mountain stood
> And the abyss grazing our cheek.

Poet of light, air, and distances, Nancy Cardozo has
some exceptional lines in "Harrier" and in "Recognitions of
Space and Time, " where she describes wild geese in flight,
"The hush of distance falling as they go. "

The section "The Cutting Garden" contains unrhymed
sonnets dedicated to her mother, and "City of Reflected
Light" recalls childhood walks in New York City with her
father. A mood piece, "Ennui, " summons up midsummer
when "the evening lasts till dawn. "

The title line comes from "Cerveteri--The Etruscan
Tombs": "In the house of death/ I wear the wind's helmet."
The later travel poems carry increased complexity, a layer
--albeit a thin one--of historical associations. They seem
less convincing than the first poems of immediate reference
and airy notation such as "Fragments from Legend":

> My body, woman,
> Diviner of suns, the moon's companion,
> Creature of water and those horizons
> Where clouds spill
> Their silver seeds.

WARREN CARRIER

Toward Montebello.   Harper, 1966, 62 pages.

In spare surreal imagery Warren Carrier does what
he says in his first poem: "On endless rides/ I race my
role, screaming from this script:/ Our dreams are true; our
lives are bitter lies. " Shifting and overlaid personae of
nightmare, myth, and fact reveal the metamorphosing hero:
"Some image or other haunts him, / Gable's last movie perhaps, / An old man struggling with horses, / Tricked by a
fatal lapse/ Of fact into duelling the sea. " There is a sense
of dream-waking ("Dead cars drone at eighty through a night/
where towns lean westward in forgotten dew") in which time
speeds up like a film ("We orbit our lives in a frenzy" and
"I whistle sonic booms").   "Big Pine" finds Carrier at play
in the fields of paradox: "if I make a mystery, Lord, / if I
see the ice and tree, / is it not to get the hang, / O Lord?
Am I not I who see?"   Implicit protest against the state of
urban man becomes explicit in "Perspectives and Recollec-
tion. " At the end, in the title poem, Crabtree Falls forms
a fusing image of the torrent of experience and of speeding
time, where for a moment the poet stands in realization:
"Against all endless falling/ Where the trout lives, and the
fisher dies. "   LJ

JOHN CIARDI

39 Poems.   Rutgers University Press, 1959, 86 pages.

Flexible modern-paced verse through which Ciardi's
voice rises above the obscurantist indulgences of critics'

poetry.   As we read we sense "the power-hum of the bees"
and "the praying shadows of stone. " Wit and a welcome
willingness to be politically engaged mark the "Ballad of
Icondic" and other poems.   However, some pieces are marred
by an unpleasant and self-conscious kind of verbal muscle-
flexing ("To Lucasta, About That War").   In the final section, "Certainties, " Ciardi's vigor and honesty place him
among the company he calls "the three truest"--Stevens, W.
C. Williams, and Frost.   "Homage to Lorca, " for example,
employs a fresh synaptic shorthand along with lines of ease
and lucid music such as "man's mystery is to sweeten his
own death. "   LJ

SAMUEL TAYLOR COLERIDGE   (about)

The Dark Night of Samuel Taylor Coleridge by Marshall
Edward Suther.   Columbia University Press, 1958, 232 pages.

    Mr. Suther considers the reasons for Coleridge's
"great failure, " that is, his early virtual severance from inspired creation.   He examines the poet's preoccupations with
philosophy and theology, and his emotional problems, but
omits opium addiction as sufficiently treated by others, and
the psychoanalytical level of interpretation as outside his own
range though relevant "if we do not fall into the reduction
fallacy. " His study centers in "Dejection: an Ode" as the
"artistic record of the major crisis in Coleridge's poetic
life. " An excellent chapter on imagery traces recurring
clusters: the storm of poetic creativity, the moon-world of
imagination, half-light as the atmosphere in which poetic experience occurs.   With some reliance on Jacques Maritain,
the distinction between poetic experience and artistic elabo-

ration is pursued.   From an acute religious need, the author
believes, Coleridge ultimately asked from poetry, as he had
from human love, more than it could give--"something cate-
gorically different"--so that his poetry offers a record of
search for the absolute, comparable most revealingly not with
English but continental writing, and especially Rimbaud. LJ

HELEN CORKE

Songs of Autumn and Other Poems.   University of Texas
Press, 1960, 71 pages.

    These period pieces, elegiac in tone, were mostly
written forty to fifty years before publication.   They derive
adventitious interest from the author's friendship (when both
were young teachers in England) with D. H. Lawrence, who
tried to rouse her from the grief of a personal tragedy out
of which the poems grew.   (That tragedy also became the
subject of Lawrence's novel The Trespassers and Miss
Corke's own Neutral Ground, and Lawrence wrote his Helen
poems to the author.)   "Prayer for the Dead" closes a cycle
of verse to "Siegmund, " from the memory of whose suicide
D. H. L. could not divert her: "Unto the God of the Dead, a
cry from the Living, / for the Dead--who cannot pray--/
Peace in thy hidden place, and a long night, giving/ no dream
of a long gone day!"   One poem is addressed "to D. H. L. "
and he shares the dedication.   Handsomely turned out by the
University of Texas Press, the book was a gift to the
Lawrence Fellowship of the University of New Mexico, which
has sponsored scholarships for young artists on the Lawrence
ranch.   LJ

MALCOLM COWLEY

Blue Juniata: Collected Poems.   Viking, 1968, 149 pages.

    These are the poems from those written across his
fifty years as a literary historian and man of letters that
Malcolm Cowley selected to save.   The title is that of his
first book of poems, which appeared in 1929.

    The Juniata is a river in west-central Pennsylvania,
where Cowley spent his early years.   "Blue Juniata, " a
ballad about it, was popular a century ago, and old-timers
still hummed it when the author was young.

    Divided into seven sections--the Pennsylvania boyhood
and mining country, expatriate years, New York during the
depression when Cowley was literary editor of The New Republic, etc. --this collection constitutes a poetic autobiography.
"Each of the sections contains new poems and old poems, "
Cowley writes.   Five of the sections are introduced by prose
notes which establish theme and tone.

    At the beginning, with "Boy in the Sunlight, " and at
the end with "Here with the Long Grass Ripening" (dated
1968), the poet's own voice comes direct and simple, free
of modes and fashions which elsewhere make of the book an
itinerary of styles as well as a personal record.   The latter
poem closes:

         I pray for this:
         to walk as humbly on the earth as my father and
              mother did;
         to greatly love a few;
         to love the earth, to be sparing of what it yields,
         and not to leave it poorer for my long presence;
         to speak some words in patterns that will be remem-
              ered.

    In between come the Eliotic stance ("The Beach at
Palavas" and others), jazz doings ("Memphis Johnny"), and

proletarian odes ("For St. Bartholomew's Eve, August 23, 1927"). These seem like exhibits in literary history by comparison. Among personalities there are a view of "Ezra Pound at the Hotel Jacob" and a glimpse of Hart Crane in the reminiscent "The Flower and the Leaf."

Cowley's best poems breathe a nostalgia that must have grown from the pervasive American sense of impermanence, no deep roots, and the marks of the westward drift across the midcountry--homes and farms abandoned because of economic failure or just to move on. "The Blown Door" is such a poem:

> Nobody nailed a new slat on the corncrib;
>   nobody mowed the hay
> or swung a gate that sagged on rusty hinges.
> The farm died when the two boys went away,
> or lived until the lame old man was buried.
>   I came then, and once more
> to see how sumac overspread the pasture,
> to smell dead leaves and hear a gust of wind
> somewhere inside the house blow shut a door.

"The Long Voyage" and "The Urn" are among lyrics which will surely hold their own. Cowley closes his collection with the latter:

> Wanderers outside the gates, in hollow
> landscapes without memory, we carry
> each of us an urn of native soil. . . .

VICTOR HERNANDEZ CRUZ

Snaps.   Random, 1968, 135 pages.

The title, Snaps, suggests the snapshot, vanishing, drug-happening sequences of this first book by a young poet, born in Puerto Rico, who lives in and writes about the New York black ghetto. Cruz unribbons a free fall, automatic

verse ("again scream/ again come/ marching in space/ do
it all/ listen/ finger finger who/ wha").   "Born To Be
Burned" is one of the effective pieces in a book which is
largely notes toward poetry.   LJ

RUBEN DARIO

Selected Poems of Ruben Dario, translated by Lysander
Kemp.   University of Texas Press, 1965, 149 pages.

        At Buenos Aires in 1933, speaking at a joint tribute
to Dario, Neruda said: "Federico Garcia Lorca, a Spaniard,
and I, a Chilean, dedicate the honors bestowed on us today
to that great shadow ... who saluted, in a new voice, the
Argentinian soil that we now tread. " That tribute (the book's
epilogue) and its prologue by Octavio Paz, condensed from
his long essay on Dario and Modernism, set Kemp's translations within a frame of appreciative evaluation.   In search
of a "modern, cosmopolitan language, " two Latin-American
Modernist movements arose between 1880 and 1910, owing
much respectively to the French Parnassians and Symbolists.
Bridging the two, Dario emerged as a kind of Ezra Pound,
both inspirer and critic, and like him a self-exiled traveler.
From "Blue" to "Poem of Autumn, " Paz says, his poetic development led and corresponded to that of the movement; and
Paz finds in him at times the "otherworldly music" of Poe,
at times the "vitalist affirmations" of Whitman.   Kemp, in
his translator's note, says he attempted to convey the "feel"
of Dario in "readable English" and omitted some important,
as he included some minor, poems according to his criterion.   LJ

PETER DAVISON

<u>Pretending To Be Asleep.</u>   Atheneum, 1970, 53 pages.

Peter Davison's verse illustrates the values of formal
limits in an art and in an era notorious for the disappearance
of limits.   His new book displays a quiet, responsible crafts-
manship.

> Searching out of pain
>   At first, then out of habit,
> And out of self at last,
>   I stumbled on surprises
> And managed to record them.

Such lines in their clarity and balanced care suggest
an accomplished ease.   Their faults parallel their virtues.
Davison's precise but casual stance can appear artificial and
studied.

Literary derivations show in a sprinkling of epigraphs
and the easy intrusion into the poet's own stanzas of lines
from Yeats and this from Wyatt: "It shuns me now that
sometime did me seek. "

Anyhow, the ear should be grateful.   The flaws of a
maker who respects his art belong in a different league from
the runaway typewriters tapping out the automatic, anonymous voice which dominates poetry today.

The quality of life concerns Davison.   His subject in
"The Gun Hand" is endemic violence--mindless assassination,
Vietnam, the eye-splitting offerings of television.   "Visions
and Voices" mourns Robert Kennedy.   "The Pleaders" points
to those who cannot speak.

"A Word in Your Ear on Behalf of Indifference, "
simple and aphoristic, leads on to the social role of the
"Plausible Man. "

"Words for My Father" (the poet Edward Davison),

like the title piece, worries the conditions and efficacious-
ness of writing poetry.   "Words need not always fail, " the
son says in conclusion; "Your gift to me is my gift to you. "

Now director of the Atlantic Monthly Press in Boston, Davison published two earlier volumes: The Breaking of
the Day (1964) and The City and the Island (1965).

Poetry that refuses to raise its voice and mistake itself for oratory may compel the listener rather than over-
whelm him.   Having to listen in order to overhear can re-
vivify discrimination, which in the past has been the gift of
poetry.

BABETTE DEUTSCH

The Collected Poems of Babette Deutsch.   Doubleday, 1969,
230 pages.

Babette Deutsch, nearing seventy-five, included in her
Collected Poems an extensive selection from eight earlier
books, a section each of translations and light verse, and
ten new poems written since her collection of 1963.

"Stranger than the Worst, " the first of the new and
opening poems, achieves a majesty beyond the reach of
younger writers and beyond any other effort of her own. The
last of its three stanzas may send readers after the full
poem:

> Yet there is something comes
> And goes, but comes again--
> Emboldening, like drums,
> But with the light grace of song,
> And stranger than the worst.
> Pure blitheness, out of the scums
> Of evil and anguish will burst

> Into a glory that
> Dazzles beyond all wrong.
> Love, as the old know love.
> Fibred with grief, it is strong.

A lifelong New Yorker, Miss Deutsch (married to
Avrahm Yarmolinsky) writes with sure and precise craft
about a thunderstorm on Riverside Drive, tugboats, gulls,
zoo animals, city occasions, and the color and weight of
days and seasons in the park. The afternoon of a July day
"sways like an elephant, wears/ His smooth grey hide, displays his somnolent grace. "

Her deftness in description can be sampled in
"Lizard at Pompeii":

> Little finger of fiery green, it
> flickers over stone.   Waits
> in a weed's shadow.
> Flashes in emerald--
> is gone.

Miss Deutsch's translations--especially those from the
Russian, such as Pasternak's "The Urals for the First Time"
--try to reproduce the structure as well as the sense of their
originals.

Social currents run strong (as in "Exodus 1947").
And Miss Deutsch who, for all her obvious commitment,
gives the impression of detached observation, writes well
and often about other artists and poets--Mozart, Braque,
Klee, Picasso, Cezanne, Stevens, Dylan Thomas, in honor
of Marianne Moore's seventy-fifth birthday. "Heard in Old
Age, " written for Robert Frost, speaks also for herself:

> Is there a song left, then, for aged voices?
> They are worse than cracked: half throttled by the
>   thumbs
> Of hard self-knowledge. To the old, dawn comes
> With ache of loss, wit, cold absence of choices...
> Till the Enigma, in a wandering phrase,
> Offers a strain never audible before:
> Immense music beyond a closing door.

DENIS DEVLIN

Selected Poems. Holt, 1963, 106 pages.

Irish poet and diplomat Denis Devlin died in 1959 at
51, leaving about 60 poems. Of these, 42 have been selected
and introduced by his friends, the poet-critics Allen Tate and
Robert Penn Warren. Though Devlin's subjects often are
Irish, he is not, the editors insist, an Irish poet but European like Valery or St. -John Perse. Among some indifferent,
a number of good and "perhaps three great poems, " they
rank one, "Lough Derg, " with Stevens' "Sunday Morning"
and Eliot's "Gerontion" as a poem of modern religious consciousness and conflict. Somewhat inadequately, they say it
"has its unique obscurities. " This is, indeed, a special
poetry of personal shorthand and telescoped syntax: compressed, dense, hermetic, with occasional vivid imagery:
"Bring the light with ropes of shaken rain, " and "Webs of
wet gaslight thread the streets and lanes. "   LJ

JAMES DICKEY

The Eye-Beaters, Blood, Victory, Madness, Buckhead and
Mercy. Doubleday, 1970, 63 pages.

James Dickey's turbulent title names a half-dozen of
the poems, and indicates something of the themes and free
fall manner of his book. Line spacing, open punctuation and
word placement aim at kinesthetic effects.
An action writer prepared to enact the major outer as
well as inner dramas of contemporary experience, Dickey
first published the "Apollo" moon flight poems in Life magazine. He received the National Book Award for his Buck-

dancer's Choice in 1966.   That's a remarkable double inas-
much as the judges usually have had an intuition of poetic
value, whereas Life usually celebrated with such versifiers
as Leonard Cohen and Rod McKuen.

Dickey begins with "Diabetes"--about his own afflic-
tion--which, he writes, has brought him "a livable death at
last. "   His voracious sensibilities erupt from within a hospital ("this night mortality wails out"), the brain of a mad
dog, or a tree.   In the last, "Pine, " he suggests the sough,
withdrawal, and continuance of wind: "nothing and then/
Soft ... sift-softening. "

His cinematic imagery seemingly flows below the
threshold of speech.

"The Eye-Beaters" describes a visit to institutionalized
blind children whose hands are tied with gauze to prevent
them from striking their sightless eyes.   Driving for affirmation out of terror, Dickey invokes a memory, "Knowing the
blind must see/ by magic or nothing. "

Sometimes his urgency becomes clinical, impersonally
magnifying or minifying the subject.

Dickey's baptism of the reader is by total immersion.
He represents the confessional trend now dominant, as in
"Turning Away: Variations on Estrangement":

> Something for a long time has gone wrong,
>   Got in between this you and that other
> And now here you must turn away.
>
> Beyond! Beyond! Another life moves
>   In numbing clarity begins
> By looking out the simple-minded window,
>   The face untimely relieved
> Of living the expression of its love.

If this poetry is often manic (exultation "with or without delusion"), it must be called mantic too (having the "gift

of divination"). With a Wolfeian appetite, James Dickey
appears to be living his poetry "where it's at" today.

EMILY DICKINSON (about)

The Years and Hours of Emily Dickinson, edited by Jay
Leyda. Yale, 1960, 2 vols., 1000 pages.

The editor of The Melville Log (1951) has prepared a
similar documentary biography of Emily Dickinson, without
comments of his own, by juxtaposing items from the poet's
own and others' letters, and extracts from newspapers and
current literature read by her. A sequential pattern results,
rich in clues to the climate and texture of her immediate
world, for the reader himself to pursue. Emily Dickinson's
pithy sentence bursts have the angled vision and often the
rhythm of her poems ("The supper of the heart is when the
guest is gone"). Vol. 1 carries from her parents' engage-
ment in 1828 to 1860 when the poet was 30 (her dates: 1830-
1886). Vol. 2 includes 1862, the year of her greatest output, crisis of the heart, and decision in her maturity as a
poet to forego recognition. Increasingly a recluse, though
hers was the "first family" of Amherst, she wore white from
this time on. (T. W. Higginson, recipient of her "Master"
letters, visited her and wrote, "I never was with anyone who
drained my nerve power so much." A Mark Twain lecture
at Amherst in 1871 was reported as "a first-class failure";
the mind boggles at a possible confrontation which did not of
course occur.) This self-illuminating continuity, indispens-
able for students of Emily Dickinson, should stand beside
Thomas H. Johnson's careful editions first of The Poems
(1955) and then The Letters (1958), each published in three

EDWARD DORN

Gunslinger, Book 1.   Black Sparrow Press, 1968, 52 pages.

A mythic gunfighter "of impeccable personal smooth-
ness" and his casual, card-playing horse meet the narrator
in Mesilla, the horse's hooves "covered with the alkali/ of
the enormous space/ between here and formerly. " Insulted
by an intruder in Lil's bar, the Turned On Horse observes,
"not looking up": "Stranger you got a pliable lip/ you might
get yourself described/ if you keep on. " The Gunslinger
makes his draw of magic speed; dialog ensues which transmutes Western clichés to high and hard rhetoric; and, joined
by a drifter and Lil, the principals take a stage out of town:
"But from Mesilla said I/ to Las Vegas--Vegas! the Turned
On Horse corrected. " Edward Dorn has undertaken a tersely
implicative narrative poem distinguished for its control and
glow of condensation.   LJ

KEITH DOUGLAS

Collected Poems.   159 pages.
Alamein to Zem Zem.   152 pages.   Both Chilmark, 1966.

These two volumes constitute the collected works of a
young English poet killed in Normandy at 24 in June 1944
after having fought as a Crusader tank leader from Alamein
to Wadi Zem Zem in Tunisia, surviving wounds from a land
mine in Palestine.   His keen participant's record of armored
warfare in the desert--its elations, fears, and tedium--is

replete with the rapid living sketches of an artist: faces of
the dead, the varied noises and babble of battle, an aid sta-
tion scene (which reminds him of Cruikshank), the emptiness
of desert and starlight.

An earlier (1946) edition of the Alamein record carried the Middle East poems as a supplement. The Collected
Poems represents a revision of the 1951 (also English) edition, with corrections and notes, chronological arrangement,
and addition of one poem and the poet's drawings. Douglas'
poetry, from "Schooldays" at 14 to his death only a decade
later, reveals technical mastery from the first. Writing in
conventional forms, the poet sometimes suggests Wilfred
Owen (as in "Landscape with Figures, " both in the form with
its slant rime and the burning pity of war). The poetry
grows more flexible and more severe through sections "Oxford, " "Army: England, " and "The Middle East" (with its
lovely lyric, "I Listen to the Desert Wind"). Douglas' most
anthologized "Simplify Me When I'm Dead" stands among
nearly equal achievements.   LJ

RICHARD EBERHART

Collected Poems, 1930-1960.   Oxford University Press,
1960,   228 pages.

The mystery of imagination returns every experience
upon which Eberhart reflects, from bombing to chestnuts
fallen, as if through a singular sunglass, clear and simple
but intensified.   His compressed colloquial language, in
appearance open and improvised, is charged with energetic
control.   "The Groundhog" and "The Fury of Aerial Bom-
bardment" belong among the best poetry of our century.

Selection from eight volumes since 1930, and fifty-one new
poems not published before in a book, are gathered here. A
brief quotation may sample one of the briefer poems, "A
Soldier Rejects His Times...": "Think no more of me/ For
I am gone/ Where ages go, / No touch of snow/ Nor sing-
song bird sip song/ Alters meadow." The poems of a
seer.   <u>LJ</u>

LOREN EISELEY

<u>Notes of an Alchemist.</u>   Scribners, 1972, 125 pages.

In these poems, jotted into his field notebooks over
the years, Loren Eiseley writes: "I am a student of night-
fall, I claim no other profession." A professor of anthropology at the University of Pennsylvania, Eiseley confirms
in "Notes of an Alchemist" the predilection for darkness,
caves and burrows previously recorded in his autobiographical
<u>The Night Country.</u>
    Appropriately, it's in "The Bats" that he makes re-
ligious supplication on behalf of all groping lives:

> Oh God forgive us doubts,
> within this fallen fractionated world of night's
>   creation bring
> all brown leaves to the universal leaf,
> all tigers, yellow-eyed,
> to where the tiger is....

Not surprisingly, then, this caring cataloger of owls,
woodchucks, butterflies, as well as artifacts turned up on the
great plains of his boyhood, says ruefully in "The Last
Days": "Sometimes I think of defecting.... Animals are
beginning to look better than my own kind. I request trans-
fer."

A toy lion still kept on a shelf above his desk suggests that the boy was father to the man. "The Face of the Lion" exemplifies the intrusion into many of the poems of a diluting sentimentality, as "The Striders" does a tendency to overplay metaphors: "Man too is a strider over light and air/ but darkness waits below. "

Eiseley writes most poetically when he records observations of natural science without extension other than the sense of wonder which preserves them.   In these his alchemy succeeds.   When he turns from animal to man he prefers the prehistoric, as in "The Olmeca, " or the Western past of his forebears, as in "Oregon Trail. "   A solitary Thoreauvian scholar, he gives the back of his hand to the protesting young in "Confrontation. "

The most ambitious poem in this collection concerns his habit, as an anthropology teacher, of taking a frayed rope to class.   "The Rope" represents evolutionary climbing, "that code of DNA, " the indissoluble but raveled links to the past; and Eiseley throws in a comparison with the rope trick of Indian fakirs.

With a fervor compounded of awe and doubt--and with some rhetorical straining--he concludes the poem in terms reminiscent of his notable early book The Immense Journey:

> Believe, oh do believe;
> look up, the rope is there
> lent by that devious double agent, night.
> Oh now we know
> the rope is hidden in ourselves to climb.

Notes of an Alchemist has been handsomely published in a gift-book format with illustrations by Laszlo Kibinyi.

GUNNAR EKELOF

Selected Poems by Gunnar Ekelof, translated by W. H. Auden
and Leif Sjoberg; introduction by Goran Printz-Pahlson.
Pantheon, 1972, 141 pages.

    In these translations, taken from two volumes in a
series known as the "Byzantine triptych, " W. H. Auden
and Leif Sjoberg have demonstrated that Gunnar Ekelof's
poetry can register effectively outside his own Swedish language.
    Ekelof, one of Sweden's leading modern writers al-
though little known in America, completed the Byzantine
triptych not long before he died in 1968.   The books from
which Auden and Sjoberg have drawn are the first two in the
series, Diwan Over the Prince of Emgion and The Tale of
Fatumeh.   The first concerns an 11th-century political prisoner released after having been tortured and blinded, the
second a courtesan expelled from the Harem at Erechtheion
into a wandering, miserable old age.
    Though he was absorbed in Oriental mysticism, Ekelof
saw these poems as speaking to our modern Western situa-
tion.   He described "Diwan" as "a symbol of the political
decadence we see around us, " and "Fatumeh" as "a symbol
of the degradation, the coldness between persons. "
    The first poem in "Fatumeh" offers a good example
of the severe reductionism of Ekelof's manner as well as his
characteristic use of paradox:

            In the autumn or the spring--
            What difference does that make?
            In youth or old age--
            What does it matter?
            In any case You disappear
            Into the image of the Whole
            You have vanished, You vanished

Now or the moment before
Or a thousand years ago
But Your disappearance
Remains.

The blind wanderer in "Emgion" habitually speaks the
language of paradox: "How blind we are when our eyes are
open"; "It is from Death that you have emerged--And life is
slowly effacing you. "

This notion of effacement also is paradoxical. Ekelof
would erase the layers of civilization and the accretions of
personal experience down to common impersonal sources. So
in "Xoanon" (which means a Greek temple icon, an ancient
wooden image) the earth mother icon is stripped of its
"basma" or protective silver shield and of its veil, then dis-
assembled. At the core the poet comes to "a piece of old
olive wood saved long ago" and finds himself watched by an
eye almost hidden in the wood, "the eye-knot of a twig. "

Here Ekelof's debt to surrealism shows itself. He
introduced French Surrealism into Sweden, with a special interest in Robert Desnos. It shows again, associated with
sight, in "A bird with observant eyes":

The lives of birds are hard:
They look at you and are afraid.

The Tale of Fatumeh plays everywhere upon shadow,
"The Shadow that lives without Sun and Moon, " the nothingness to be embraced. The Shadow asks the poet, "At your
place? Or at mine?" He has already responded with a
metaphysical shudder: "I see who you are. It is for you to
take me. "

During his final illness with cancer Ekelof observed
that he "rests his case on nothingness. " Yet the Shadow
also represents the omnipresent feminine principle in these
poems: "Nothing, You tender and merciful One, Who place

men's hands in one another. "   So, for final paradox, "The
merciful She gives what she does not give. "

T. S. ELIOT

Collected Poems, 1909-1962.   Harcourt, 1963, 221 pages.

Published for T. S. Eliot's seventy-fifth birthday, this
volume holds "all of his poetry through 1962 that he wishes
to preserve, " from "Prufrock" to "Four Quartets. "   A final
section, "Occasional Verses, " contains five pieces: "Defense
of the Islands" and two others are concerned with wartime
events; all are limited to topical or biographical interest and
written in the tutorial rhetoric that sometimes afflicted
Eliot's later manner.   The main begetter of the poetic sensibility of his own age, Eliot undertook not only to appraise
its ailments but to "redeem the time. "   And that progression
may be followed from the landmark symbol, "The Waste
Land, " through the suggestive metrical hesitancies and acute
lyric beauty of the pivotal "Ash Wednesday, " to his later
more discursive and public speech, in this presentation of
the most influential poetry of our century to date.   LJ

T. S. ELIOT   (about)

Notes on Some Figures Behind T. S. Eliot, by Herbert
Howarth.   Houghton, 1964, 396 pages.

These "Notes" make a chronological record of influences upon Eliot and probable sources for his ideas and
forms.   Among much incidental Americana we learn that the
St. Louis of his childhood had already produced "a circum-

ambience favorable to the growth of genius, " with an educa-
tional debt to his father. Other indelible places would include Gloucester and London. Eliot knew Harvard in the
"golden era" of James, Santayana, Royce, Kittredge, Bab-
bitt especially: men upon whose ideas (together with some
less well remembered) he drew for half a century of creative
work. He took with him Petronius and Dante. Then came
the "transforming discovery" of Laforgue; Maurras ("clas-
sique, catholique, monarchique"); Pound's "rescue" from philosophy for poetry; emergence of the cinematographic form
of "The Waste Land"; long effort to attain a "transparent
poetry" and a modern dramatic speech restoring the diction
of conversation; seventeen years' editorship of The Criterion
as a British mediator for Europe and between Europe and the
world: the incubating sensibilities of Joyce, Arnold, Hof-
mannsthal, Beethoven. After a slow seedbed start, Howarth
has given readers of Eliot an illuminating study, packed and
yet digestible.   LJ

PAUL ENGLE AND JOSEPH LANGLAND   (editors)

Poet's Choice.   Dial, 1962, 303 pages.

    This anthology prepared by Paul Engle and Joseph
Langland represents 103 poets writing in English.   Each was
asked for his favorite from his own work and to give reasons
for his choice.   The signature of each poet is reproduced,
and there is a section of "Brief Biographies" arranged, like
the poems, chronologically.   Inclusions range from Frost and
Graves to Ginsberg and Levertov.   Eliot, Sitwell and Auden
preferred not to choose, and George Barker pokes fun along
with his quatrain.   On the other hand, Aiken, Warren,

Nemerov are very serious and have very long choices.
Whereas Thom Gunn chooses "The Sad Captains" because it
came easy, Spender and Graves choose pieces because they
were difficult.   Shapiro asks, "Why must grown people listen
to rhymes?"   But Ciardi asks, "How can one fail to be happy
about singing?"   Like Ferlinghetti, many name not "the" but
"a" favorite, often a recent composition.   Or the selection
may have meant a turning point for the poet, like Louis
Simpson's "Walt Whitman at Bear Mountain."   Naturally a
lot of good poems got in and the volume is of general interest.   LJ

ESKIMO POEMS

Anerca, edited by Edmund Carpenter.   Dent, 1959, 48 pages.

        Simple songs and chants of Eskimo daily experience,
the hunt, berry-picking, the beauty of light, and death, these
are both old and new, and all anonymous.   Carpenter writes:
"In Eskimo the word to make poetry is the word to breathe;
both are derivatives of anerca, the soul. ... " Drawings of
the chase and journeying are by Enooesweetok (Baffin Island,
1913-14), collected by the late Robert Flaherty, producer of
Nanook of the North.   Most of the poems are untitled; the
first, "Great grief came over me--, " can be found in slightly
different form in the poetry appendix to Rockwell Kent's
N by E (1930).   This version continues: "Great grief came
over me, / While on the fell above us I was picking berries. /
Great grief came over me/ My sun quickly rose over it. "
Origins of translations are given on the final page.   LJ

DAVE ETTER

The Last Train to Prophetstown.   University of Nebraska
Press, 1968, 86 pages.

A sadness of the midwest town settling into existential
funk pervades this book.   "Back home under the dying elms,
I watch/ gnats bug the last slants of rusty sun. "   Accenting
ennui, "The train limps out of town discouraged. "   After experiencing Etter's jazz pieces with a nod to Lindsay, the
Sandburg-folksy word play of "Are you saying me?", and
occasional surrealist effects, the mind retains the shabby
trains, the "antique light, " a sense of loss (apostrophes to
Ann Rutledge, Altgeld, Adlai Stevenson), forsaken one-room
schools, and the empty persisting enclosing fields.   Etter's
gift is the evocative, indigenous imagery: "Above the porch
light, crusty with bugs, / grape leaves rattle in a damp
wind. "   LJ

ABBIE HUSTON EVANS

Fact of Crystal.   Harcourt, 1961, 48 pages.

The title poem and much of what follows celebrate the
miraculous emergence of life, the gift of identity haunted by
the sea.   Elemental fact and experience come sheer in lyrics
of natural ease and authority.   The first excellence is sharp
perception: the robin's "colored note for rain, " or sunrise
"Behind the wattle of the alder swamp. "   The image-unlock-
ing word is in its place--"implicated, " for instance, in "Old
ocean's hoarse and implicated roaring. "   Lyric stanza and
blank verse carry varied music from one "with my bones of
rock-dust hardly knitted/ And my blood still salt from the sea. "
                                                                  LJ

FRANCIS FERGUSSON / CHARLES NORMAN

Poems: 1929-1961, by Francis Fergusson.   Rutgers University Press, 1962, 130 pages.

Selected Poems, by Charles Norman.   Macmillan, 1962, 91
pages.

    Fergusson's verse collection is the first by a writer
well known for dramatic and literary criticism.   It spans
over thirty years, and early inclusions ("Mrs. White, " "The
Blumenscheins.... ")--sardonic, fragmentary, with tag allu-
sions--have their debt to Eliot.   Later, originality speaks,
as in the eloquently moving memorial poem "On the Turning
Earth. "   "Penelope, a Theater Lyric, " a verse play, takes
almost half the book.
    Norman's Selected Poems also go back to 1929, the
year of his first collection.   Early poems well reflect the
Imagists ("The Thin Rain":   "The stumbling elephant of wind/
Lunges against the stacks of rain.... ").   Later come Yeats-
like condensation and directness.   (For example, "The Bright
Meadows, " "To a Certain Critic. ")   Many poems concern
the wars and travails of three decades.   Rather than intensity,
they reveal a talent for refined song.   LJ

ROBERT FITZGERALD

Spring Shade.   New Directions, 1971, 192 pages.

    The earlier poems in Robert Fitzgerald's harvest of
40 years, all carefully crafted, may look and sound like
period pieces today.   "The Shore of Life" with its tone of a
weary urban tawdriness brings back memories of the '30s,
the diction and pacing shared with T. S. Eliot or Archibald

MacLeish:

> There the hot taxis at the pounding corner
> Fitted their glossy flanks and shifted, waiting,
> And the girls went by with wavering tall walking,
> Their combed heads nodding in the evening:
> The hour of shops closing, the cocktail hour,
> Lighting desire and cigarettes....

Fitzgerald's own individual notes are thin but clear, in the tranquil imagery of "Sea Pieces," for example:

> Low sun, a cooler light
> Exhaled; low evening stains
> Waterblue under beeches.
> The longlegged children
> Are furling their sails
> In the air like clear water,
> The water like air, like mist.

Such pieces with their clean delicate simplicity suggest watercolor. It is as an imagist of classic temper that Fitzgerald appears at his best.

"Portrait," one of his quotable poems, describes John Wheelwright's effort

> To write a sterner myth than Tate's
> Or that of Cummings or of Crane--
> Owned and disowned the Concord gates
> And Cousin Brooks's sweet terrain.

As Boylston Professor of Rhetoric at Harvard the poet has lived part of each year at Perugia, Italy. Several Italian sonnets brim with the Mediterranean world and its associations.

> Far from New England's leafiness I write
> In that land of the old latinity
> And golden air.

Fitzgerald received the Bollingen Award in 1961 for his translation of the Odyssey. Spring Shade closes with a selection from his versions of Virgil, Catullus, Horace, Villon, Perse, Borges and others.

His themes emphasize concern for the conditions of a

livable meditative life: "the gay abnegation that is grace";
"the simplifying diligence of honor"; "good instruction and
delight. "

ARTHUR FREEMAN

Estrangements.   Harcourt, 1966, 52 pages.

This is the second book of poems by Freeman, on
the faculty at Boston University.   (His Apollonian Poems
appeared in 1961.)   His verse has highly civilized and formal
manners with its intimations, allusions, and ironies.   "The
Dog Far Hence" describes a "transparent, skeletal fish/
propped among the pebbles, its grin and eyes/ peopled with
flies, " and "Drink Me" or "Interior" applies a similar
imagistic deftness to the social realm.   There are lines that
recall Donne, and the Browningesque "Beauty, Sleeping, " and
best of all, occasional lines of direct appeal such as "The
clear air tightens like a fist" ("Autumn").   By comparison
the long penultimate "The Occupation, " dealing with Germany,
seems contrived.   LJ

BARNABE GOOGE

Selected Poems of Barnabe Googe, edited & with introduction
by Alan Stephens.   Swallow, 1961, 61 pages.

"In the stiff courtly convention, the subject and the
attitudes are assumed at the outset, " writes Alan Stephens,
introducing the seventh in Alan Swallow's "Books of the Renaissance Series, " a distinct service to the student of poetry.
Googe, a minor artificer within this tradition, typified Eng-

lish poetic style between Wyatt and Spenser. Influenced by
Tottel's Miscellany, exercising its "formulary rhetoric, " he
wrote occasional pieces and lyrics in alliterative "four-
teeners" or endstopped pentameters. The selection was made
from his Eclogues, Epitaphs, and Sonnets, published first in
1563 and long out of print. The editor has modernized
spelling and punctuation.   LJ

ROBERT GRAVES

Collected Poems. Doubleday, 1961, 358 pages.

        Graves, as all the book world knows, is a carefully
careless ("I have never written a poem in less than three
drafts") Anglo-Irish all-purpose writer, two decades domiciled
in Spain at this writing, whose creative pose is that of the
omnicompetent (5 Pens in Hand) classics-drenched tough Last
Romantic. His closing poem here, "Leaving the Rest Un-
said, " stops "At a careless comma, ". Erudite, easy, frequently charming, always lucid, often shallow running, this
is his fifth collected poems, once again eliminating the un-
satisfactory. A selected poems omitting such pedestrians as
"At the Savoy Chapel" would do better for cleanly shaped
poems such as "To Juan at the Winter Solstice. " Classic,
medieval, Welsh and Irish themes ("Cry Faugh!" with Yeats'
stance: "Proud remnants of a visionary race!"), and satire
for these times and for academic knowledge; "The Face in
the Mirror" says of himself in age: "He still stands ready,
with a boy's presumption, / To court the queen in her high
silk pavilion. " This can fairly be called the poetry of prose,
occasional, discursive, Apollonian, seldom magical, but ex-
pert even in whimsy.   LJ

HORACE GREGORY

Medusa in Gramercy Park.   Macmillan, 1961, 65 pages.

Richly detailed settings bathed in the gold light of history and myth, technical ease, metaphysical curiosity and
ironic comprehension mark these monodramas of the solitary
consciousness which in form and mood continue a long development by the poet with roots in the '20s and '30s. United
by their tone of muted or impending tragedy, the "Dramatic
Episodes and Lyrics" making up most of the volume (the
last section is called "Allegories and Parables") present a
modern crisis-tempered commentary in classical and Renaissance stage settings with an open end upon space-time and
change.   Among the best are two shorter pieces from the
second section, "Goethe Aetat 83: Eckermann Speaks" and
"On a Celtic Mask by Henry Moore. "   LJ

CHARLES GULLANS

Arrivals and Departures.   University of Minnesota Press,
1962, 76 pages.

Charles Gullans, teaching at UCLA, appropriately de-
dicates his book to Yvor Winters, addressed in "Some California Wines": "Dear Winters, it is right your songs/ Be
honored by the land in this, / Both sweet and full, true flavor
for true tongues/ That speak what is. " Supple under conventional forms, the poems trend to epigram; some are
translations from Rilke, Petrarch, etc.   Best are the love
poems, and the final long one in blank verse, "An Old
Woman ... 1919, " sustained with beauty.   They least appeal
when didactic, as in "Return Voyage, 1955, " an overspoken

generalized piece. Three are about current poetry: "The
New American Poetry" swings at the Beats; "The Second
Draft; or, Slouching to Byzantium" belabors academicians
with Yeatsian parody; the last, "A New Scots Poem" in dia-
lect, does little for Gullans and nothing at all to minify Hugh
MacDiarmid. Poems of Augustan lucidity and balance, with
pirouettes of wit.   LJ

RAMON GUTHRIE

Asbestos Phoenix.   Funk & Wagnalls, 1968, 132 pages.

    "There is one story and one story only, " elder poet
Robert Graves declares, "that will prove worth your telling."
Ramon Guthrie, a kindred tough Romantic of Graves' vintage,
tells it in his lead poem, "Suite by the River. " In it he
hopefully casts a love spell over Melusine in retaliation for
her younger charms, which include "the feral low tonalities
of your unprecedented voice in darkness. "
    Explaining the title Asbestos Phoenix, Guthrie writes:
"An underlying theme of the book is that I and most other
sentient humans are non-combustible Phoenixes. " Our in-
ability to enact the myth, he says, and be reborn from our
own ashes makes of life a pointless tragedy.
    Confronting the intolerable, Guthrie turns on a clown's
disarming face and riddles experience with wit and word delight.   "Cantata for Saint Budoc's Day, " with allusion to a
Breton saint transported from Ireland on a floating stone,
flaunts a joyous rhetoric:

    Harrook, old hamster, you honk-nosed janissary!
    Hindle me not, ye horehounds, Lest ye'd be holystoned.
    Harrook! Can't ye not see I'm hasping down the halyards?
    Harrook, ye meddlestrums. Unhook your harps from here!

He can, as in "Wunday the Worst of Weptober, " be
most serious under the merrymaker's mask: "There is a
nightmare I must ride to where its aberrations end. "

Guthrie, born in New York, deliberately cultivated an
exotic flavor and lived much abroad, with Brittany for his
Majorca.   Self-supporting and self-taught since he was 14,
he received an honorary M. A. from Dartmouth and taught
French and comparative literature there for 35 years.

His poetry has been called "a self-portrait constantly
retouched. "   "Pattern for a Brocade Shroud: after Watteau"
retouches some more and refers to military service in both
World Wars and in the "punitive expedition" against Mexico.
But the book climaxes with poems of indignant social protest.
"Scherzo for a Dirge" describes a despairing letter from a
conscientious objector to the Vietnam War.   "Postlude for
Goya" (1938)--one of two inclusions written before 1959--re-
calls, as still central, the death of Republican Spain:

> We cannot win--though we perhaps have won
> if we can only believe
> that this is not the end.

"Why should not old men be mad?"   Guthrie assents
to that rhetorical question of Yeats.   It can be expected that,
like Whitman, he will remain "garrulous to the very last, "
sometimes nearly a relic voice refurbishing personae from
the expatriate generation.

Occasionally he sinks to the banal, for instance at the
close of "It Happens, " about the incidence of a kind of tran-
scendental love: "Oh I too could sometimes shout or sing or
sob wild hosannas to its name. "

"Marsyas in the Intensive Care Ward, " a hospital-
stay poem, refers to the myth wherein Marsyas challenged
Apollo, the god of music and poetry, to a musical contest.

He lost, of course, and was flayed alive for his presumption. In "Marsyas, " upon his timeless themes of time and love, Guthrie writes at his characteristic best:

> Gamut of goddesses, Gaia, Latona, Frigg whose day it is,
>   cat-flanked Ishtar with the up-turned palms.
> Rosmertha of the Gauls, with grief-gauged eyes...
> Intercede for me.   Let me be never born.
> Let my ghost wander in brambled upland meadows.
> Drizzle in evening streets, may she at times recall
> our walking there, arms pressed to ribs together.

RAMON GUTHRIE

Maximum Security Ward.   Farrar, Straus & Giroux, 1970, 143 pages.

Lying in the intensive care ward of a hospital, Ramon Guthrie noted its numbing or horrifying correspondences with the "maximum security ward" of his title.   He enlarges the theme outside hospital walls until it encompasses universal human experience.

Hospital details are set down with grisly humor:

> Lash him firmly to the stretcher
> and store him in the ghast house for the night.

Interwoven are reminiscences of two world wars and of the expatriate years which Guthrie, 75 at this writing, spent in Paris:

> Montparnasse
> that I shall never see again, the Montparnasse
> of Joyce and Pound, Stein, Stella Bowen,
> Little Zadkine, Giacometti ... all gone in any case,
> and would I might have died, been buried there.

"Fiercer than Evening Wolves" recounts the violent blasphemy of his believing mother on her deathbed, almost dehumanized by a series of strokes.

Thematically, the first part of the book documents the poet's assertion that he would rather have been born a dog, "Would never have opted to be human." Part Two makes a partial retraction.

Here, among images of death and pain, Guthrie lies pondering the "christoi," his personal heroes of action and art. "Self-anointed" by their dedication, they include the prehistoric cave painter of Lascaux; "Einstein, Rembrandt, Blake, Louise Michel, innocence that may be contagious." Because of them the poet reconciles himself to his humanity.

A grudging, hard-won, skeptical faith shows in "People Walking," about a Parisian antiwar march in which he joined:

> They are good people...
> They have faith without hope
> or hope without faith.

The final poem celebrates an intuition of permanence perceived in glimmers through the transcendence of art. The strong "The Making of the Bear" evokes and describes a primitive cave painter's ordeal as he attempts to reach beyond himself. The last poem, "High Abyss," concerns the performance of a Beethoven string quartet:

> I have come back having grasped perhaps as much
> as a lightning bug, clinging through a storm
> to a leaf's underside,
> might understand by fellow-feeling
> of a lightning stroke that in a single blast
> has ripped the elm trunk all its length.

Ramon Guthrie writes in a timeless manner, traditional but free, with direct vigor. At times only a strain of sentimentality touches a false note. Throughout the book, stitching the short poems which compose it into a whole, run binding motifs: the aging poet's plea to a younger Melusine who doesn't write to him; the myth of Marsyas, carried over from the poet's previous volume, The Asbestos Phoenix

(1968); such heroes of the Left and the Resistance as Robert
Desnos; the ordeal and transcendence of art, and above all,
"the christoi":

> the named and unnamed, the forgotten, though not less
>   close for that,
> the unknown, the dead who are living their fullest lives now:
>
> Louise Michel with her great spate of love--
> and hate where hate was needed. Stendhal, "hussard
> de la liberté. " They who made
> Falstaff and Charlus, Hulot, Pickwick.

MICHAEL HAMBURGER

Weather and Season.   Atheneum, 1963, 64 pages.

Hamburger, who has been on the faculty of the University of Reading in England, has translated several books
of German poetry and this is his own fourth book of verse.
He underplays it, usually. "Omens" begins "The year opens
with frozen pipes, / Roads impassable, cars immovable, " to
end with casual horror: "Next year I shall see no meadow,
no horse. " Quiet elevation to eloquence comes "In a Cold
Season" about the poet's grandmother who died in Nazi Germany, and about Eichmann: "But show him pity now for
pity's sake/ And for their sake who died for lack of pity... /
Dare break one word and words may yet be whole. " Bitterly
honest, preoccupied with the social and political weather of
our mortal season, the lyrics also often fix impressions of
"The Moment": "It was the angle:/ Sunlight, and how it
fell. "   LJ

MARC HAMMOND

The Horse Opera and Other Poems.   Ohio State University
Press, 1966, 85 pages.

"The Horse Opera, "   about the Western as American
myth (Cooper and Gable "Rode stallions through the mountains
of our dreams"), brings on solo a familiar cast: The Bad-
man (for Jack Palance), Barkeep, Old Prospector, Rebel
Soldier, etc.   For all Professor Hammond's talent, though,
this rates as ho-hum, sometimes perfunctory and banal.
"Darwiniana, " in which monkeys "Talked and walked together
and were men, " suggests the sonnets of Auden.   What's done
is Donne in "Atlantis III":   "And we would live there, careless who/ We were some days ago or will become. "   Iowa-
born, Hammond convinces in midwest poems such as "Sub-
urban Nocturne, " which imagines a band of Indian hunters
where homes now stand, one of whom "leapt with the deer to
a deeper forest/ And dark, deadlocked in branches and ant-
lers, / Awoke, astonished, to hunt among the stars. " Here
myth is kindled.   LJ

MARCIA HANS

Serve Me a Slice of Moon.   Harcourt, 1965, 58 pages.

Busied with extraction of essences--of apples, snow,
moon, flight, sound (one to a poem)--Marcia Hans' poems
yield crisp images like the rainy night's "patent-leather
streets" with cars moving "on narrow stilts/ of/ light. "
They have the concentration of haiku: "Lightning--/ a careless rip/ in the sky's clothes, / that shows/ for a second, /
its gleaming-white/ bare/ back. " This concentration can

slacken into cuteness, "Nothing smells as green as green, "
or the word "dizzily" dispersed vertically down a page.
Better the kittenish work-play of "snice" for sleety snow or
the fanciful gallery guard who disappears into a blue painting.   The title poem ("Serve me a slice of moon/ on a hot
summer day") suggests early Sandburg.   A poetry of perceptive improvisations.   LJ

CHRISTOPHER HASSALL

Bell Harry and Other Poems.   Harcourt, 1964, 43 pages.

       Bell Harry, central tower of Canterbury Cathedral,
could be seen from the author's garden (he died in April
1963) and it broods above these poems of meditation on loss
and nature.   Part one, a sequence of forty traditional sonnets in memory of Frances Cornford, Hassall's poet-friend,
follows changes of the year with reminiscences of her last
illness and of their readings together among sights and sounds
of the English countryside.   Moving through doubt (death is
"The monstrous platitude of passing time"), they attain a reconciliation with nature in the final sonnet, about coming upon
a well: "And peace was standing there like waiting water. "
Part two, with freer forms, confirms the impression of a
sensitively receptive mind, remote but accurate in observation, precision-skilled in verse.   LJ

RALPH HODGSON

The Skylark and Other Poems.   St. Martin's Press, 1960,
86 pages.

Nearly forgotten as a minor Georgian poet, Ralph
Hodgson, 88 at this publication, and his 20-year American
residence on an Ohio farm, came to public attention with
The Skylark. A bibliographic note by Colin Fenton, who
edited the privately printed London edition in 1958, records
six poems printed for the first time; the remainder include
all of Hodgson's published verse since Poems in 1917. The
title poem was written in 1910 and one piece, "Portable
Wireless, " as recently as 1955. Brief and in ballad meters
mostly, spontaneous though unoriginal, this is the work of a
pure lyricist with a permanent if modest place among English
poets. "The Skylark, " second stanza, reads: "A later skylark takes the sky, / A wiser world lies under;/ And still
we put our wisdom by/ And give the bird our wonder. " Indignation at human cruelty to animals and indifference to
nature pervades this as it does the earlier verse, and provides the theme for the long, incomplete, "Muse and the
Mastiff. " The magic of "Time, You Old Gypsy Man" or
"Eve" from the 1917 Poems has no equal in this later book.
Some lyrics and fragments are wholly colloquial though em-
ploying quaint diction, and the older Hodgson runs to epigram.   LJ

JOHN HOLMES

The Fortune Teller. Harper, 1961, 96 pages.

By the New England poet-teacher, these are poems
mainly of family and occupation. They are of two kinds.
The first, home-made and colloquial, run to homily ("Cow
Be Killed" or "Holiday with Gods"). With ambling line and
clear statement, they are often nostalgic, with a saving

facetiousness as in "Carry Me Back" and "My Old Schools, "
the latter ending: "when the cold edge comes too close,
humor is an insulation. " The lyrics, on the other hand, are
Housman-stripped and tight, "Death in the Back Yard" and
"Letter to My Mother" among the best. Their lean phrasing
balances Holmes' general tendency to garrulity as if sometimes he would take poetry by force of words. Holmes (who
includes a poem each to Frost and Eberhart) is nevertheless
a craftsman working to embody the fugitive suggestions of
tone and mood and implication that wait just beyond everyday
experience.   LJ

EDWIN HONIG

The Gazabos: Forty-One Poems.   Clarke & Way, 1959, 57
pages.

     The gazabos, like Yeats' circus animals, are the
poet's obsessions--"my worn out longings, / my poems that
dog me/ till I die. " Honig's verse, condensed and masculine, brims with force and bounce--as in "Outer Drive"
with its glimpse at the city's homegoing hour of "a sudden
snub-cabbed truck, trailerless, / Intense; like a bullhead
bodiless it rockets. " A steady vision informs an often car-
toonlike imagery: "Gabbing crows ... rear/ and plop,
chuckle swivel-/ headed, peck/ the meadow dead. " It becomes explicit in "Pray Eros" which quotes Pound ("What
thou lov'st well/ Remains, the rest is dross") and adds:
"Up, beast in heart. / Can you burn till you're the nugget
of that song?"   LJ

TED HUGHES

Wodwo.   Harper & Row, 1967, 184 pages.

Ted Hughes is a Yorkshire nature poet whose somber
energy can be sampled in "Skylarks":

> My idleness curdles
> Seeing the lark labour near its cloud
> Scrambling
> In a nightmare difficulty
> Up through the nothing
> Its feathers thrash, its heart must be drumming like
>   a motor,
> ... Wings almost torn off backwards--far up

Immersed in a nature and striving which he sees as
brutal, barbed and undeflectable, Hughes thinks with his blood
as he listens for "below words, / Meanings that will not part
from the rock. "

"The Howling of Wolves" calls up "The eyes that never
learn how it has come about/ That they must live like this,"
while "Gnat-Psalm" describes the insects

> Weaving and bobbing on the nothing
> Shaken in the air, shaken, shaken
> And their feet dangling like the feet of victims

The "victims" strewn everywhere are Hughes' persis-
tent theme.   Midway in the book four Kafka-like stories and
a black expressionist playlet, "The Wound, " comment on and
have their counterparts in the poetry.

The poem "Out, " about a father mutilated by war,
makes a reduction of "The Wound" in a similar episode, "As
after being blasted to bits/ The reassembled infantryman/
Tentatively totters out, gazing around with the eyes/ Of an
exhausted clerk. "

The characters in the stories wait, each one isolated,
with ominous foreboding, enclosed in settings dense with snow

or rain or heat. In "The Harvest" a hunter feels himself becoming the hare he has been hunting, and in "A Vegetarian, "
a parallel poem, "Unable to move, he hears the hounds of
the grass. "

    "Pibroch" renews the blind striving theme:

        A tree struggles to make leaves--
        Minute after minute, aeon after aeon,
        Nothing lets up or develops.

No darker verbiage has been sown in recent English
verse. Ted Hughes may have become the toughest, strongest
poet writing in England during the decade since his first
volume, The Hawk in the Rain, came out in 1957.

    "Wodwo" (wood-troll), the title poem closing Hughes'
book, a kind of "Song of Myself" in reverse, asks: "What am
I? Nosing here, turning leaves over/ Following a faint stain
on the air to the river's edge. " Like the hero of "Sir Gawain
and the Green Knight, " from which his title comes, "Sometimes with snakes he was, and with wolves also.... Both
with bulls and bears. "

RICHARD F. HUGO

A Run of Jacks. University of Minnesota, 1961, 72 pages.

    The poems in Hugo's first book are full of the north
Pacific coast around Seattle where he lives. Many first
appeared in Poetry and the literary quarterlies. "Trout"
shows a strong fresh exactness, the moment's hard reflection
given in free syllabic meter: "Quick and yet he moves like
silt.... / ...he carved the water into many/ kinds of current with his nerve-edged nose. " Sometimes speed of imagery
dissolves the short lines in fury of restraint, or underwater

identification brings the unreal.   Occasionally an effect
misses, as in "Snoqualmie":   "Southless birds/ decline to
sing. "   Usually verbal rediscovery and redeployment work
their miracle: the "sky is weak from light"; "water rolls to
the shore like surly ground. "   LJ

INDIA (SELECTED POEMS)

Poems from India, selected by Daisy Aldan.   Crowell, 1969,
158 pages.

        Daisy Aldan, who teaches in the New York City High
School of Art and Design, has met a number of the selected
poets of her volume in their native India or in this country.
Hers is the third in Crowell's "Poems of the World" series
which includes Poems from France and Poems from the German.   Miss Aldan's collection, illustrated by Joseph Low,
provides a sampler from the long, vast poetic literature of
the subcontinent.   Intended especially for young people, it
ranges from the aphoristic psalms through the classical San-
skrit into the tang of modern speech, in poems written directly in English and others translated from 14 regional language groups.
        From the Mahabharata, one of India's two epics along
with the Ramayana, has come the "Bhagavid Gita, " the "Sublime Song. "   (These epics are compared roughly with the
Iliad and the Odyssey.)   Krishna, an incarnation of the god
Vishnu, counsels Arjuna:
        There is no tranquility for a person who will not contemplate:
        and there is no bliss without tranquility.
        Sanskrit court poetry from India's middle ages may be
savored from "Summer" by Bana:

In this summer month which blasts all hope,
Burns the vines, is angry at the deer,
Is tree-wilting, bee-distressing, jasmine-hating,
Dries up lakes, heats dust and fries the sky;
In this month that glows with cruel rays,
How can you, traveler, walk and live?

Kalidasa, sometimes called the Shakespeare of India, is represented by an excerpt from "The Cloud Messenger. " The much more widely known Rabindranath Tagore, recipient of the Nobel Prize for Literature in 1913, translated his own "On the Seashore" from the original Bengali.

After absorption of British influences in the nineteenth century, the national movement, culminating in 1947 with independence, brought a poetry of social consciousness. Rao, for example, writes of "the green fingers of the sun freezing" in "Elegy for a Dead Child in the Street. "

As in the West, recent poetry emphasizes personal search and uses rhythms and vocabulary influenced by expressionism, surrealism, symbolism, the legacies of Eliot and the "Beats. "

Writing in English about her native India, Mary Erulkar closes movingly and suggestively:

And in the strangers' hearths where the golds of gold sing
While the smell of new bread swings from the windows,
All night the women's dreams cry like mice;
And in the moon-hung orchards of sleep the children laugh
Before the apple-red and hungry mornings rise.

JOSEPHINE JACOBSEN

The Animal Indise. Ohio University Press, 1966, 113 pages.

Josephine Jacobsen observes carefully and writes fastidiously. She describes the "Fiddler Crab" in motion: "He raised a notch and ran/ in tippity packy glide to the

wave's wink. " In "Country Bath" the June bug comes against
"the raw bulb hanging/ ... thutter and thutter and soft pop
deadly. " Her richness of rhythm is Hopkins-like and infrequently found in poetry today, as in "Delire des Profundeurs"
with its "sea's light of noon, / In the slowmotion silence and
sliding slip.... " The elegant, punctilious speech of such
poems as "The Autopsy" (the neat shudder of "When she saw
him next he was most formal") has recurrent lush Haitian
pieces for counterpoint. The title comes from a passage in
The Golden Bough: "The animal inside the animal ... is the
soul. "   LJ

ROBINSON JEFFERS

The Beginning and the End and Other Poems.   Random, 1963,
74 pages.

In his last poems Jeffers' themes are unchanged,
though more personalized, probably because of the death of
his wife Una.   The powerful, inhumanistic, dark-shining verse
places human experience in the atomic age in minute scale
beside "The Great Wound"--the "myth" of the moon being torn
from its Pacific cradle--and the tides of oceans and stars.
The first section, "The Root of All Things, " traces human
evolution within the more enduring transhuman scheme.   "The
Great Explosion" sums up: "And we, God's apes--or tragic
children--share in the beauty.   We see it above our torment,
that's what life's for. "   "Do You Still Make War?" depicts
man the self-slayer.   "Memoranda, " among other themes,
celebrates intuition over logic and scientific method.   The
final section, "Autobiographical, " has the intensely sad resignation of "Cremation" (for Una); "Granddaughter" (named Una

also), invoking for her "the beauty of transhuman things, /
Without which we are all lost. " "The Shears" shows some
relenting, placing man in, rather than opposed to, nature.
But "Animula" says the last word for Jeffers: "the billion
light-years cause a serene and wholesome deflation. " The
impressive final poems of a great poet.   LJ

WALTER KAUFMANN

Cain and Other Poems.   Doubleday, 1962, 190 pages.

A Princeton professor of philosophy, Kaufmann lived
as a Jewish boy in Nazi Germany.   These poems--skeptical,
sad, honest--reflect both his vocation and that experience.
He writes in "What Weighs?": "Auschwitz' smokestacks/
dwarf one Jew on the cross/ and the death of god. "   And in
"They": "Freedom and doubt are twins. "   Typically, his
"Portrait of a Lady" (very unlike Eliot's) has for setting a
postwar interrogation center in Germany.   Ranging from reflections on nature to the horror of genocide, frequently with
Bible figures and themes, this work does not always succeed
as poetry but it has such satiric gems as "Father Feeney. " LJ

WELDON KEES

The Collected Poems of Weldon Kees.   University of Nebraska
Press, 1962, 186 pages.

Weldon Kees, who committed suicide in 1955 at 41
from the Golden Gate Bridge, was not only a poet but an abstract expressionist painter (he once exhibited with de Koon-
ing and Hans Hofmann, subject of a poem), a jazz pianist,

and a Hollywood film-maker.   The depression years in which
he grew up unrooted (starting on the Federal Writers' Project
in Lincoln), and the following war, darken poems now little
known.   Indeed Rexroth wrote: "Kees lived in a permanent
hopeless apocalypse. "   These incomplete Collected Poems are
drawn from three volumes, periodicals, and some manu-
scripts.   Unoriginal in style, their burden of bitterness rises
with recurrence to "an overwhelming question. "   Looking
back, the suicidal note is insistent as in "The Fall of the
Magicians":   "It is good to be deaf in a deafening time... /
And let the world's black lying flag come down. "   LJ

ROBERT KELLY

Finding the Measure.   Black Sparrow Press, 1968, 123 pages.

        Kelly's shorthand syntax and cryptic allusiveness sug-
gest Pound, without discredit.   His "prefix" gives the clue to
line and theme: "Style is death.   Finding the measure is
finding/   a freedom from that death, a way out, a move-
ment/   forward. "   A subtle, accomplished poet, he brings
aesthetic pleasure and sometimes puzzlement in "the finding":
"Battering at the gates.   Wet moon. /   A maniac/   goes to
let them in.   Moon hands on us.   The door. "   One of Kelly's
best, "for G:L: & T:M:" mingles Egypt, the ibis god, Ohio
caves: "I thought I heard old Horus say/   my sun is set/
I die into this other... /   Into your dream I pour/   the number of the secret word/   that kills us all. "   There is syllable
play ("sudden Krakatoa/ of the cock's/ crow/ a"), and, in
"Who attends another's business, " too many parentheses,
asides, sound-leadings.   The avid poetry reader will gladly
go along as this poet finds his measure, his "mantram. "   LJ

X. J. KENNEDY

Growing into Love. Doubleday, 1969, 96 pages.

     X. J. Kennedy adapts conventional measures to the
tempo of today. He sounds like a knowing observer and participant, adept and wry, even when in this second volume,
Growing into Love, he opts at moments for dropping out of
the modern scene.

     "The Medium Is the Message" asks not whether the
teenager is turned on, but rather to what:

> Fresh beats the age insists on, not the heart's,
> But those of rush-hour traffic's fits and starts.

     The poet-teacher adds his own concern "Lest one word
of Yeats lapse. "

     Emphasis on the grotesque, a note of strangeness,
enter the familiar stuff of daily headlines and talk--freeway
motorcycle accident, man in space, best seller, "Loose
Woman, " with its violence and sex-murder in Dallas.

     Kennedy reveals occasional updated echoes of "Don
Juan, " Housman, Robinson, and--more directly--of Edwin
Honig's The Gazabos and of Lowell's early manner: "The
bird broods on a setting of brown stone" ("Requiem in Ho-
boken").

     The homogenized anonymity of an American tourist,
perpetual prey to highway and motel, revisits the cringing
reader of "Driving Cross Country":

> A room the same as last night's room,
> Exact same bath mat underfoot,
> In thrall to some unlucky charm,
> We hurtle; but, it seems, stay put.

     Most of the poems collected here appeared in The
Atlantic, The New Yorker, Poetry, Hudson Review and other
magazines. Kennedy's first book, Nude Descending a Stair-

case, was a Lamont Poetry Selection.

Technical proficiency amply shows itself on these pages. The verse rises above proficiency, and above the surface flippancies, as timely, responsive and responsible poetry.

STANLEY KIESEL

The Pearl Is a Hardened Sinner: Notes from Kindergarten. Scribner's, 1968, 76 pages.

Out of his 14 years of kindergarten teaching in Los Angeles, Stanley Kiesel has sketched an album of five-year-olds. The reportorial jottings of their traits and doings are invested with tenderness and with dismay.

"I see you. " he writes to Kim, "nagging the gravel with your feet ... Did you keep the pebbles/ In hopes that they would mother you?"

Kiesel often relies on paradox to translate his hard look into verse: "The ill, rebelliously ill children, remind me/ Of men out of work; and so they are, out of play. " He may strain for an image but fix it in an aphoristic profile, as he does in "Belinda":

> This culturally-deprived
> Mexican child dances
> Upon nothing.   Fortunately
> Joy has no need of soap
> Or water--nor a ribbon
> In its hair (children
> Are its ribbons)....

Criticism of bland and blind assumptions pursued by teacher, parent, social worker, registers less effect in the somewhat unctuous moralizing of "Postgraduate" than when implicit in the portraits.   We find a teacher whose "intentions are to see that Blue/ Is never painted next to Green. / And

that the sexes use separate toilets. " And a social worker
"Who sicks her knowledge on you like a dog. "

"Miss R" gets more extended and sympathetic treat-
ment. A spinster teacher devoted to one of her passing
pupils, she has little except "the television she drank from
like a bottle. " For her, in lines of sudden lyricism: "Over
the soiled rags of the sky, / Sailed the tuneless flotilla of the
rain. " In a poem with a related theme Kiesel writes to
Gregory, a homeless child, "I was only guaranteed for one
year. "

Irrepressible life skips forth in Jamie as in Belinda:

Snowman of mirth, small hired hand, erase the board...
It is not important to discover what you celebrate...
The joy in you, Jamie, is a certificate of birth for
    everyone.

Some of these warm and wry poems appeared in Contact and in San Francisco Review, although this is Kiesel's
first book. Its revelations about a kindergarten world alive--
and lived through by children--deliver affection, indignation,
twists of irony, sharp bites of truth.

CAROLYN KIZER

The Ungrateful Garden. Indiana University Press, 1961, 84
pages.

"The metaphor, like love, / Springs from the very sep-
arateness of things. " The author extracts poetry from contemporary events, bits of memory, language itself, with
supple play. In her title poem Midas concludes, after "Gold
thorn has made his fingers bleed, " that "Nature is evil. " The
fantasy of "By the Riverside" emerges from a telephone di-
rectory's injunction: "Do not call from memory--all numbers

have changed. " "The Death of a Public Servant" expresses indignation at the suicide of an envoy falsely accused of being "unAmerican. " Two lyrics, "The Great Blue Heron" and "What the Bones Knew, " approach the stripped richness of Yeats. The love poems have a clear lack of inhibition. There are three translations from "A Heine Journal" and several tankas "In the Japanese Mode. " Clear sophisticated poems. LJ

JOHN KNOEPFLE

Rivers into Islands. University of Chicago Press, 1965, 55 pages.

Most of the poetry in this first book, written in the understated, tense contemporary mode, first appeared in the quarterlies. It derives from the border between Midwest and South where Knoepfle has taught English and tape-recorded old rivermen's memories. Infrequent jubilance ("rebel rabble-rousing banjos") relieves taciturn notations about the late shift at a mill, pensioners on a park bench, a keelboatman's horn. There's grotesquerie ("Harpe's head") and folklore ("The white mule": "they have known it under the earth, / heard the hoof-beats ranging the pits... "). Knoepfle's pithy lyricism is at its best in "Country night": "Alone on the bluff/ he comes in quiet. / The bluntheaded owl/ has wind for wings, / his eyes two imperceptible moons. " These are poems of hard-won brevity, compassionate, sardonic, still.   LJ

KENNETH KOCH

Ko, or A Season on Earth. Grove, 1959, 115 pages.

In mock-Byronic stanzas, this bizarre narrative paro-
dying the romantic epic-length poem shifts from Ko, newly-
signed Dodger pitcher from Japan, to Andrews, to others, in
a perpetual triple play of plot, Tucson to Tibet, the strings
being jerked together in conclusion after criss-crossing.
"Meanwhile" introduces switches at the most inopportune
moments.   One of the author's five cantos could have made
the possible point about pointlessness.   Item: "So for ten
years he grew in fog and blizzard" (Wordsworth, takeoff on).
Item: from stands in ballgame, "hear the fizz/ Of mountain-
goatca-cola" (if reach p. 111).   A doggedly tedious satire and
exercise in odd-rhyme virtuosity.   LJ

WILLIAM R. LAMPPA

In Familiar Fields with Old Friends.   Branden Press, 1972,
127 pages.

William Lamppa's poems deal with scenes and characters among the woodland farms of northern Minnesota around
Embarrass, where the author grew up.   They are simple, un-
adorned and as unpretentious as the soft-bound format in
which they are published.

Many of the 121 inclusions, dating from 1956, have
appeared in newspapers and little magazines.   Most are short
and pervaded with nostalgia.   "Lost, " the final poem, expresses the recorder's predominant mood; the reader's reflex
is toward the need for a sense of community, of connected-
ness with other people and the surrounding land.

Typically, "Just Waiting" describes the old folks when
the young are gone, sitting by themselves in their farm
kitchen.   Their elbows "rest on a checkerboard tablecloth as

the clock ticks relentlessly behind a dusty sunbeam. "

Nostalgia marks the visit to a boyhood shanty, the sight of a deserted schoolyard, memories of blueberry picking and haymaking, a survivor glimpsed living his leftover life in "Remaining on the Farm, " and a mother left solitary again the day after Christmas. A few poems admit sentimentality when eyes blur or the speaker seems "to have a speck of dirt in my eye. "

But others strike wry notes: "Inside Out" recounts a thwarted romance. Horror or fantasy touches "Among the Dripping Roses, " in which a skeleton beckons, and "They Are Here Now. "

Direct and indirect protest of the Vietnam War is the theme of half a dozen brief poems. One, called simply "Vietnam, " expresses the pathos of children attempting normal play near huts that have been scorched by napalm.

The poet's naturalism and level voice make their best appearance in "First Snow Storm" and in "The Night of the Swamp. " Here is the latter in its entirety:

> Night sinks darkly
> into dimming pines,
> and rolls overhead like
> a dream of black thunder
> in slow motion,
> while hunched rabbits settle,
> shifting weight from
> one hind foot to the other,
> and continue nibbling
> in the darkness.

Although not a "literary" writer, Lamppa momentarily suggests Stephen Crane's "The Black Riders" in the fugitive horsemen of "Where Issues Are Decided, " and he recalls E. A. Robinson in "Adrian, " about a lonely drinker on a moonlit hilltop above a sleeping village.

But he generally tells it straight out, as it is and was

in the northern reaches of the North Star country.

IRVING LAYTON

A Red Carpet for the Sun.   Jonathan Williams, 1959, un-
paged.

        This poet, prominent among the Toronto "Contact
Group, " styles himself an anti-Romantic and one of the roughs.
His verse is notable for energy and sharp observation (as in
his description of a frog as "Chaplin-footed") but frequently
adds too much and uneven comment.   Verbal exhibitionism
includes much sexual allusion and many tough words.   "The
Puma's Tooth" gives the typical burden of his thought: "Man's
a crazed ape/ A balled-up parasite. " He has included,
among "all the poems I wrote between 1942 and 1958 that I
wish to preserve" some fatuous rhymes about Marilyn Monroe
entitled "Earth Goddess" ("There is more wisdom/ In your
shapely bum"), but is far better in the taut stanzas of "Poem
for the Next Century" and "Parting, " which take a Yeatsian
posture.   LJ

DENISE LEVERTOV / ELEANOR ROSS TAYLOR

Footprints, by Denise Levertov.   New Directions, 1972, 58
pages.

Welcome Eumenides, by Eleanor Ross Taylor. Braziller,
1972, 55 pages.

        Among the volumes of poetry published in 1972, two
books by women, Denise Levertov's Footprints and Eleanor
Ross Taylor's Welcome Eumenides, are exceptional productions.

Both possess technical mastery and persuasive idiom.

Ms. Levertov has published frequently over a decade and a half, as an ardent spokeswoman for the alternate culture. By contrast, Ms. Taylor has not had a book since her first publication, Wilderness of Ladies, in 1960. Her stoical, exacting, pithy style will probably continue to mean a relatively small readership in the future.

Stony with loss and death, most of her poems exert a chilling influence. From "Song":

> Don't go to sleep, I cry,
> Now gray--but can I know
> The stupefaction of all losses?
> In your suspended face
> No flicker shows
> If you remember me, or care,
> Or will come back.

Her two longer pieces, which concern war and death, are based upon diary entries made by the principals, extended in strict notation by the poet. "A Few Days in the South in February" concerns a Civil War incident in which a Union father traveled to Charleston to bring home the body of his son: a reconstruction etched in pathos.

The central piece, "Welcome Eumenides, " draws its title from a diary entry by Florence Nightingale, narrator and subject of the poem. Recording her resolute acceptance of terror and pity in Crimean hospital wards, this exercise in anguish seems to reduce experience to an epitaph, a severe winnowing of time and life.

By coincidence, Denise Levertov's "The Malice of Innocence" deals with memories of her own experience as a hospital aide, "lost in the death room awhile ... crudely, cruelly in love with order" and "writing details of agony carefully into the Night Report. "

Ms. Levertov's new poems are "natural numbers, "

further testimonials on behalf of resistance to life-denying
forces whether political or ecological.   There's a higher incidence than in her earlier books of immersion in the non-
human, the life of trees or birds.

      Evocative, tender, mature, these poems reveal a wist-
fulness of middle age reflecting, with a Cassandra note to the
young: "Can you be warned?"   "February Evening in Boston,
1971" captures the shine on ordinary things as "People are
quickly, buoyantly crossing the Common/ into evening, into/
a world of promises. "

      In a tone very different from that of <u>Welcome Eume-
nides</u> ("O God no more love no more marriage"), Denise
Levertov continues,

> It was the custom of my tribe to speak and sing;
> not only to share the present, breath and sight,
>   but to the unborn.
> Still, even now, we reach out toward survivors.   It
>   is a covenant of desire.

DENISE LEVERTOV

<u>Relearning the Alphabet</u>.   New Directions, 1970, 121 pages.

      In this collection Denise Levertov appears as both poet
and activist.   The wife of Mitchell Goodman, a co-defendant
in the Spock trial, she has been "relearning the alphabet" in
middle age to read aright this troubled era.

      "From a Notebook: October '68-May '69" concerns in
part the Berkeley People's Park confrontation between Es-
tablishment and counter-culture: "What people can do--be in
the streets--they're ours!"   "Biafra" shows how hard it is to
write an editorial poem.   Topicality and humane heavy-heart-
edness pull it toward prose.

   Like Shelley, this technician of light and grace beats
"luminous wings" of social concern.   But we may reflect that
today it tells us more about Matthew Arnold than about Shelley
that Arnold thought his wings beat in vain.

   Ms. Levertov's grace and light are here in simple
natural images:

   I watched the blue iris leaning under the rain,
   the flames of the poppies guttered and went out.

Hers has been the most successful effort after William Carlos
Williams in his "variable foot" or breath rhythm.   And like
Williams', hers has to be an individual conquest.   Breath or
phrase rhythm is simply too personal to sustain a valid prosodic theory.

   This poet has given a healthy reinfusion of speech
idiom to poetry. But diffuseness signalizes the technical
problem.   "Dance Memories," with its rhyme and half-rhyme,
appears to sound her own sense of this.   Such prosodic reg-
ularities constitute the book's most interesting technical aspect
and may count in "purifying the language of the tribe" some
day.

   The music and matter of a poem ought to be one.
Ideally, neither the maker nor the listener would disjoin them.
In Relearning the Alphabet Denise Levertov, a poet neither
immature nor frivolous, proposes as Shelley did that her society should move to a different drummer.

DENISE LEVERTOV

With Eyes at the Back of Our Heads.   New Directions, 1959,
74 pages.

   "It's not a question of/ false constraints--but/ to move

well and get somewhere/ wear shoes that fit. " That defines
the voice of Denise Levertov.   Born in London, now a New
Yorker, prominent among the "new avant-garde, " she was
first published by City Lights Books (Here and Now, 1957)
and Jonathan Williams (Overland to the Islands, 1958).   She
writes an intense shorthand of objective perceptions infused
with a sharp sense of now.   Often on domestic themes, always fresh, her poems have ease and poise without affecta-
tion.   Yet they are artful and personal too.   She domesticates
imagination in "The Five-Day Rain, " after watching the hanging wash above long coarse grass seen through "fine shreds"
of rain: "Wear scarlet! Tear the green lemons/ off the
trees! I don't want/ to forget who I am, what has burned
in me.... "   LJ

PETER LEVI, S. J.

The Gravel Ponds.   Macmillan, 1960, 59 pages.

      Peter Levi, S. J. , a Catholic English poet, sets down
in lines taut, clear and musical a sombre beauty of nature
and the doom of innocence ("A tightening net/ traps all creatures").   The insistent note of his gravely passionate first
book is sadness: "Never, O never in the long distraction/ of
the heart's inaction, / never will a cry shake/ that prison, or
wildness wake. " With true catholicity he writes poems for
both Robert Frost and Gregory Corso.   His language like
Yeats' is distilled from common speech as in this wry epigram: "The lads of course arrived too late, / but still, for
a small fee/ --Christ being already crucified--/ they chopped
down the tree. " Peter Levi writes that he has learned from
Hopkins' "negative virtues" and that his master is Horace.

Though published in English magazines, he and his richly restrained poems are too little known in the United States.   LJ

JOHN LOGAN

Ghosts of the Heart.   University of Chicago Press, 1960, 79
pages.

        Ghosts of the Heart are summoned most persuasively
in John Logan's intimate poems of experience such as "The
Picnic, " written in flexible five-stress lines about an experience in youth.   It condenses the space and atmosphere of a
remembered day.   "The Brothers: Two Saltimbanques" describes boys balancing themselves on a train and also comes
fresh and clear.   The more cryptic manner of "The Lives of
the Poet" with its sparer line shows in frequent literary allusion, epigraphs, and terminal tracings of poems' ancestry
such as "After a definition of Xenocrates and a poem of
Richard Eberhart and after lines of Eliot and Alejandro Car-
rion. "   A verbal mixture of the formal and colloquial isn't
resolved in fusion, but does suggest that Logan works toward
this resolution.   A Catholic poet, he celebrates creation with
a rather austere ecstasy: "Ah God, if Christ has not a body
as/ The student (and the older) artist does, / And all of that,
what good is He to us?"   Logan, who has taught at Notre
Dame, wrote A Cycle for Mother Cabrini and has published
often in periodicals.   LJ

DICK LOURIE

The Dreamtelephone. New Books, 1968, 43 pages.

Lourie's phone-calls from "The Longlost, " "The Sweetchick" and others proceed in a macabre vernacular while "the hooded operator/ malevolent as cats/ listened with her teeth. " He writes more cheerfully of New York Eastsiders "lined up next to their cars like camel drivers" in Sunday washing ritual, as their island area floats off, children singing, toward Puerto Rico in the sun. His occasions of protest as a child welfare worker and his anti-war "When Johnson Came To See Me" are plaintive rather than bitter. An authentic voice of our urban fix in homemade brochure format.   LJ

ROBERT LOWELL

Imitations. Farrar, 1962, 149 pages.

Translations of this order amount to new creations. As the title suggests, they are free English versions rather than literal translations, and place the spirit before the letter. Lowell's rendering of Villon combines lines from "The Legacy" and "The Testament" and leaves out topical allusions to produce a Villon for now. His clear unforced-rhyme rendition carries natural and satisfying rhythm and refrain. The "Imitations" range from a passage of Homer to Pasternak, and emphasize Mallarmé, Valéry, Baudelaire, Ungaretti, Leopardi, for a total of 66 poems. Many lines cling: "The Swan" of Baudelaire that "struck its dry wings on the cobbled street"; and in Valéry's "Helen, " "the rowers' metronome enchains the sea. " These far outdistance an occasional forced or unemphatic line ("an oasis of horror in sands of ennui"). The translation of Pasternak's "Hamlet in Russia, a Soliloquy" is especially good.   LJ

ROBERT LOWELL

Life Studies.   Farrar, 1959, 90 pages.

    Graphic personal and family history "studies" in New
England setting, these poems recall The Mills of the Kava-
naughs (1951) but with increased informality of tone and meter.
Full of people (usually Naval) and particularity, often instant
with loss ("Terminal Days ... "), they pack the poet's habitual
verbal density, crisp allusion and pictorial dexterity (a slow-
ing train's "querulous hush-hush of the wheels"; the sun-
flowers, "Pumpkins floating shoulder-high").   Period poems
with contemporary bite.   Several less personal pieces retain
the tighter, more sonorous style of the Pulitzer-prize Lord
Weary's Castle (1946).   An evocative, even fervid, prose autobiographical fragment, "91 Revere Street, " takes nearly half
the book, replete with Boston ancestry and incidents, and
childhood memories of a home "looking out on an unbuttoned
part of Beacon Hill. "   LJ

EUGENE McCARTHY

Other Things and the Aardvark.   Doubleday, 1970, 81 pages.

    Former Senator Eugene McCarthy calls these poems a
tribute to American poets who have explored beyond the
"known and certain" of human experience.

    His first two pieces celebrate Robert Lowell ("Poet-
priest of the bitter sacrament") and James Dickey.   Lowell's
poem "For Eugene McCarthy" stands as the book's introduction.

    Adepts can perceive in that opening juxtaposition the
contrast between proficient and amateur versecraft.   But an

amateur standing doesn't invariably mean ticky-tacky tidings.
These poems are usually memorable, at moments haunting.
And they have added interest in suggesting something of the
spiritual landscape explored by our one veritable masterless
politician.

Like Emerson, whom he at times resembles and who
was a quixotic craftsman himself, McCarthy at his best becomes a seer of simplicity, a maker of aphorisms.   For example, "In a Chinese Mode" and "Dogs of Santiago, " or
"Silence":

> the mocking bird
> does not mock the silence
> of other birds, its silence
> is its own.

More topical are "Vietnam Message" and "Kilroy":

> Kilroy
> whose name around the world
> was like the flag unfurled
> has run it down
> and left Saigon
> and the Mekong
> without a hero or a song
> and gone
> absent without leave
> from Vietnam.

The introductory poem by Lowell (from his Notebooks)
carries a fugitive cinematic flavor of McCarthy's great cam-
paign.   It closes:

> --the game, the passing crowds, the
> rapid young still brand your hand with
> sunflects ... coldly willing to smash the
> ball past those who bought the park.

Shall we and the "rapid young" see a renewal of those
aspirations, and if so, will he be on the scene?   All the book
answers to such speculation may be found in the last lines of
"Lament of an Aging Politician":

> I have left Act I, for involution
> and Act II.   There mired in complexity
> I cannot write Act III.

HUGH MACDIARMID

Collected Poems.   Macmillan, 1962, 498 pages.

Burns himself never surpassed several poems by Hugh
MacDiarmid (pseudonym of Christopher Grieve), Scottish na-
tionalist and literary renaissance leader, unorthodox revolu-
tionary, 70 at this publication.   In MacDiarmid's words,
"This volume does not contain all the poems I have written,
but all I think worth including in a definitive collection.   The
twelve volumes of poems I have so far published have all been
drawn upon; some of them have been included entire. "   There
is also a section of previously uncollected poems.   Some
poems are in Scots, some in English, some are "multi-
linguistic. "   Though the many obscure the best it's difficult
not to quote, and here is the first stanza of "The Eemis
Stane":   "I' the how-dumb-deid of the cauld hairst nicht/ The
warl' like an eemis stane/ Wags i' the lift;/ An' my eerie
memories fa'/ Like a yowdendrift. "   David Daiches elsewhere
rendered this as follows: "In the very dead of the cold harvest night the world, like a loose tombstone, sways in the
sky; and my awesome memories fall like a down-drive of
snow. "   The effectiveness of the Scots becomes plain, as with
Burns.   That poem, "Moonstruck, " "Wheesht, wheesht, my
foolish hert, " "Yet ha'e I Silence left"--and others--bear out
the poet's own proud statement: "I have been hailed in many
quarters as the greatest Scottish poet since Burns ... or--the
way I prefer it put--as one of a trinity with Burns and Dun-
bar.... "   Though not all the poems require it, the glossary

is inadequate. And such a poet, "multi-linguistic" at that, should have had an introduction, preferably by David Daiches (whose article "MacDiarmid and Scottish Poetry" in the July 1948 Poetry could hardly be bettered for the purpose).   LJ

C. F. MACINTYRE

Tiger of Time and Other Poems. Trident Press, 1965, 90 pages.

       C. F. MacIntyre has translated Rilke and Baudelaire among others. His own selected poems here are rich and gutty. A number are variations of the sonnet, some sestet first, with slant rhyme and assonance to take the curse off regularity. As a fellow senior poet he has the avid romantic stance of Robert Graves, but he is less tidy, less lucid, and earthier. ¡ The sense of stalking time too is everpresent, overtly so in the title poem. Lyrical, primary, colorful, bawdy, in the classic vein, this poet asks for readers who can "feel the Attic-chiseled symmetry... / pure as a young fawn/ sucking at a grape. "   LJ

LOUIS MACNEICE

Eighty-Five Poems. Oxford University Press, 1959, 128 pages.

       Of this "comprehensive selection" the author writes that they "are not, I assume, my eighty-five best poems.... My main object has been to illustrate different kinds of my work. " Never so programmatic or impersonal as were at one time others of the former Auden Circle, MacNeice has written best in subjective descriptive poems with what one

critic called "snapshot imagery": "Snow, " "Sunlight on the
Garden, " and "June Thunder, " an evocation of coming storm
pervaded with quiet emotion.   Another mode, technically seek-
ing the tune of the time, is represented in "Bar-Room Ma-
tina" and "Death of an Actress" ("Give us this day our daily
news").   MacNeice appears on the evidence of his substantial
selection as a determined artificer; the ear stands on tip-toe
for his hidden rhymes.   No doubt a group of the early poems,
including "Sunday Morning, " will continue to haunt anthologies.   LJ

FREDERICK MANFRED

Winter Count: Poems 1934-1965.   James D. Thueson, Publisher, 1966, 78 pages.

    Like the Sioux, Frederick Manfred makes a winter
count of his years, dated by happenings, inner and outer,
in his collected poetry.
    Winter Count is an offering of Minneapolis publisher
James D. Thueson, a handsome volume in which Thueson has
combined poems, format by Barbara Rohach of Eden Prairie,
and portrait by Duane Noblett, with his own perceptive skill.
    Manfred's readers will want to get this book, tracing
as it does the underground stream along the course of his development as the Upper Midland's most notable novelist.
    Whether these more formal poems excel the lyric pas-
sages embodied in Manfred's prose, readers may decide for
themselves.
    From the first poem, "The West Sends a Call" (dated
July 1934, at Calvin College in Grand Rapids), Manfred reveals himself a populist in literature.

Frequently there's the nostalgic backward look, asses-
sing (as in the title poem or "Charlie"), the language home-
spun, indifferent to canons of taste, unlicked, and strong.
He writes as if Emerson were right and "every word was
once a poem. "

Of the love poems "A Fantasy" seems most fused, with
its imagery out of country things rather than literary: "The
sun a golden tine/ Slanting through the window. "

By contrast, some poems, "Why Weeps the Willow
Tree" for instance, are marred by inversions or poeticisms.
"Four Voices in a Dream" carries alliterative hint of Frisian
or Scandinavian myth and word ordering, delighting in sound
as sense: "Mark me, I am ... grin and grimace/ groan and
greeting. "

The latest poems alternate between the mortal resig-
nation of "I Am Fifty" (and the indecorous unforgettable "Fall
Silent") and a resolute confidence in life, "Of Flesh and
Song. " The writer wants his record whole.

"The Old Black Silence, " with some magnificent chunks
embedded, concludes: "From Ylem in, hot, hard, tight, /
To Outspread out, cold, far, flown, / There's little sign of
Voice, / There's little sign of Choice. "

This "chorus" brings Hardy's Dynasts to mind.   But
Manfred works in rawer stuff, with relentless fidelity.

FREYA MANFRED

A Goldenrod Will Grow.   James D. Thueson, Publisher,
1970, 63 pages.

The years of transition from girlhood to womanhood
are commemorated in this first book of poems by Freya Man-

fred. The poems, impulsive and brooding, are shoots of awareness. They expose a grave openness to life, an unconstrained eye, and a rare verbal sensitivity.

"Visit to Wralda" describes "this child-time land" of Ms. Manfred's early home. She catches the textures of nature and has instant sympathy for small things (a black beetle "clicking your teeth into the strawberry leaves"). After seeing her cat seize a gopher she calls out to the wind's "dark dirge": "Drown for me the gopher gurgle and the clip of sharp cat teeth. "

"The Dormitory" reflects in a mirror of words the solitary and self-regardant adolescent, whose half-sorted tumult of feeling surfaces in "Against Uncare. "

"Moon Light" finds her riding "on the way to May. " And in "Love at Twenty. " the title of a book section, she tells her companion,

> Put your feet beside my feet
> in the mutter water sweet,
> put your eye before my eye,
> touch this mouth and hold this sigh. •

Among the most effective pieces are "What the Fire Takes" and "Buffalo Night. " The latter contains the lines: "feathered moon moths swept the grass, " and "great and moody horn-hooded eyes. " It achieves a mystic identity with the prairie and the prairie past.

Mostly in free rhythms and occasionally in rhyme, the poems are presented in a strikingly apposite and attractive format by James D. Thueson, the Minneapolis publisher. This title adds another to his already impressive regional list.

Freya Manfred says: "I began writing when I was four, probably in imitation of my father"--the novelist Frederick Manfred. Her second book (at least) has already been written.

A Goldenrod Will Grow constitutes a gallery of vivid
sensory details, half-held thoughts, rain and nature whimsy,
personal music. Her poetry of things and places, of the in-
vincible stemming of the goldenrod, also reveals the poet's
growth toward form: an emergence bearing its own charms
and beauty.

WILLIAM MEREDITH

The Wreck of the Thresher and Other Poems. Knopf, 1964,
48 pages.

"The Wreck of the Thresher (Lost at sea, April 10,
1963)" summons "the severe dead" in the wreck to speak:
"Now they are saying, Do not be ashamed to stay alive, /
You have dreamt nothing that we do not forgive. " With a dis-
cernible touch of "The Dry Salvages" ("Whether we give assent to shipwreck, or rage/ Is a question of temperament
and does not matter") and relaxed line and diction, the poem
ends effectively: "The ocean was salt before we crawled to
tears. " Also among Meredith's best, "Roots, " an aphoristic
blank verse dialog, introduces one of old Mrs. Leamington's
innings thus: "Her face took on the aspect of quotation. "
Most themes are from daily life: a quarreling couple, middle
age, "On Falling Asleep to Birdsong. " Attractive poetry,
perhaps too level and casual but with heightenings in intensity,
the volume closes with the restrained optimism of "Consequences": "More than I hoped to do, I do/ And more than
I deserve I get;/ What little I attend, I know/ And it argues
order more than not. "   LJ

W. S. MERWIN

Selected Translations, 1948-1968.   Atheneum, 1968, 176 pages.

This wide-ranging selection of translations, done over
twenty years, has aimed for "the greatest possible fidelity to
the original, including its sounds. " Merwin, who has largely
made his living by translating, had this precept directly from
"the great exemplar, " Pound.   The selections begin with an
anonymous Egyptian poem (20th century B. C.) and end with a
cluster by the iconoclastic young Russian Iosip Brodsky.
Peruvian, Eskimo, Vietnamese, Welsh poems accompany Li
Po, Catullus, Neruda and various others.   The exotic and
primitive poems were approached through French or Spanish
translations--the only languages in which Merwin claims proficiency.   Precise care and poetic skill appear to have sum-
moned, as he hoped, the "taste of the source" to his rendi-
tions.   LJ

W. S. MERWIN   (translator)

Some Spanish Ballads.   Abelard, 1961, 127 pages.

The Spanish romance (roughly, ballad) arose during
the 14th-century decline of poetic epic, drawing upon it, re-
calling particular events or persons, old legends such as that
of King Don Rodrigo, and, later, contemporary happenings as
well.   It tends to the direct sparse quality of oral transmis-
sion.   In Merwin's sampler, rendering sense before song, the
water of life sometimes has evaporated with translation.   The
late lyric romances are most lively, the others generally bare
lines in dry detail.   Not ballads in the Scots-English manner,

the romances relied upon implied conclusion, and formally
(in Spanish) may have had a norm line of eight syllables with
assonantal or half rhyme.   Their chief modern influence has
been on Lorca.   Merwin's selection has five divisions: Romances of 1) "the Epic Cycles, " 2) "Single, " 3) "Historical, "
4) "Moorish, " and 5) "Late Lyric" origins, with 6) "Wonder-
Mongering. "   An introduction to a little known literary area. LJ

MODERN VERSE IN ENGLISH

Modern Verse in English: 1900-1950, edited by Lord David
Cecil & Allen Tate.   Macmillan, 1958, 688 pages.

        An eminently correct gathering of poets, with ample
selections from most, this collection adheres pretty well to
its announced span, dominated according to Lord David Cecil
by neo-romanticism.   It has been hailed by professors of literature as "the best yet. "   However--so much Yvor Winters,
so little Kenneth Rexroth (reflecting the bias shown in re-
marks critical of William Carlos Williams and "the exaltation
of the common man"), no Kunitz, Rukeyser, Fearing at all,
though Tate claims some representative intention beyond his
personal choices.   The British selection omits newer voices
and is not representative of Yeats, omitting his later poems
with a single exception.   And though Tate's essay calls part
of "Little Gidding" the "high-water mark of modern poetry"
it is not included by Lord Cecil (nor is Eliot's "Ash Wednesday").   Chronological arrangement with 55 Britons and 61
Americans intermixed; more than 500 poems.   The editors
contribute introductions; that by Tate is of particular excellence and interest.   Seeing poetry at the end of a period
style, he also discusses the value of "alienation, " and the

"New" Critics' failure to see themselves as "trapped specta-
tors. "   LJ

HOWARD NEMEROV

New and Selected Poems.   University of Chicago Press, 1960,
116 pages.

     About one-fourth of this volume had not previously been
published in book form (though all 15 new poems appeared in
such magazines as The Nation, The New Yorker and Poetry).
The rest is selected from Nemerov's first four books, 1947
to 1958.   The forms most frequently used are a blank verse
oriented to speech rhythms (still freer in the recent "Life
Cycle of Common Man") and a tight fluent rhymed stanza of
the poet's own.   Of the former, often given to reflections on
nature, "Deep Woods" has Frostian ease and personal accent;
so has "The Sanctuary": "Over a ground of slate and light
gravel, / Clear water, so shallow that one can see/ The
numerous springs moving their mouths of sand. ... " "Brain-
storm" reveals a man alone in a house shaken by wind at
night, thinking as he hears the crows that "The secret might
be out:/ Houses are only trees stretched on the rack. "
Nemerov is a fresh, neat poet whose manner is urbane, witty
and sensitive; discursive too, but few practicing craftsmen in
poetry are likely to repay more readers with more pleasure.
                                                              LJ

ROBERT NYE

Darker Ends.   Hill & Wang, 1969, 64 pages.

     These are very well crafted poems, mostly on occa-

sions in the life of a young married couple. "Shadows, "
though, owes its accent to Yeats. The title piece about making shadow pictures on a wall for a small son has a Frostian
metaphysical twist ("it is no true delight/ To lie and turn the
dark to darker ends") which doesn't seem to be adequately
earned by the poem. Wryness and a gift for epigram are the
poet's own. Here is "Somewhere": "A hooping in the firs, /
A looming in the weir--/ The wind and the rain are also
lost. " Formally skillful and communicable poems, true in
their life.   LJ

PAUL OPPENHEIMER

Before a Battle and Other Poems. Harcourt, Brace & World,
1967, 50 pages.

    Paul Oppenheimer, English instructor at Hunter College,
says in his foreword that the battle of his title is "to rescue
life from abstraction. We are before the battle because,
whenever we win it, we discover that we've won it for a moment only and that the battle must be fought again. "
    It just isn't possible to agree with the publisher that
he has won the battle in his first collection of poems (some
of which appeared in The New York Times, The Literary Review and The Humanist).
    The title poem represents a fluent rehearsal of the
sonnet form, but in such secondhand diction and rhythm as
occur again in "Gauguin": "I marvel, though, not that he lived
but died. "
    The reader sometimes gets a bath in expensive rhet-
oric, for example in "Epitaph for Satan, Who Died a Sea
Captain Lost at Sea in the Year Zero. " Word orgy and in-

flationary expression are bad enough in prose but at least in
the generous novel they may cry out for room according to
their strength.

Oppenheimer's tendency to literary usage rather than
expression that seems to spring from life comes off only a
little better in the love poems, pervaded as they are by a
sense of deja vu: "An ancient music seemed to melt her
veins" (from "For a Young Woman").

The climactic "Egyptian Sonnets" are skillful but without conviction of feeling, so that the book as a whole im-
presses as an exercise in forms for poetry and not as poetry
accomplished.

ROBERT L. PETERS

Songs for a Son.   Norton, 1967, 76 pages.

In spare lines like exposed nerves the author records
memories of a dead son and sees the world through the transformation brought about by his loss: "Look. / Those trees
hold nothing/ in their branches. Those rushes/ by the
lake, so rife with/ blackbirds, hold nothing. ... " The lines
with their painstaking detail, their attempt to live back into
the small boy's experience or to share the present with him,
carry grief in the weight of their syllables ("I shall never
touch snow/ and not see your plaid coat"). The relentless-
ness of loss carries also into poems about the exigent lives
and deaths of small animals. A sensitive, moving book of
enduring memory.   LJ

WILLIAM PILLIN

Pavanne for a Fading Memory.   Swallow, 1963, 82 pages.

Early memories of the Ukraine, the writer's Jewish
heritage, and Nazi terror recalled from the U.S. open the
volume ("At night the horizon was red/ with a burning
epoch...").   The title poem and the long "Countdown" infuse
quiet, nearly delicate imagery with nostalgia and overhang it
with menace: "For decades now there is an imminence/ in
the air; a stealthy approach/ of danger on fiery forepaws...."
Often Pillin suggests an elfinized Whitman on tiptoe: "I con-
front the star-spell of the esplanades!/ I walk as jaunty as
a sailor...."   Isadora Duncan, Chopin, ceramics, creative
imagination, are subjects of the final section with its gently
wry "Prologue to a Reading":   "You do not see it?   You do
not hear it?/   Clearly, this audience/ is bewitched by un-
friendly wizards. "   LJ

HYAM PLUTZIK

Horatio.   Atheneum, 1961, 89 pages.

Plutzik's ambitious and striking narrative poem, begun
at an Air Force base in England and completed at the University of Rochester where he taught English, recounts Horatio's
loyal odyssey into old age in obedience to Hamlet's dying injunction.   Wrappings of ambiguity unwind, from rumor and
distortion immediately after the tragedy, to Faustus' abstruse
metaphysics, to a shepherd's retelling of the story as myth
fifty years later, to the final complexities of introspection in
Horatio's old age, his long effort to redeem Hamlet's "wounded

name" a failure. But had Hamlet (with ironic consequences)
merely meant to save Horatio from a "Roman death" so that
he might live out his own life? Was the play the thing?
Practical advice had come from the prime minister: Legally,
Hamlet was a regicide, with no evidence but a ghost for his
cause. While Horatio lived in the past, the State must adapt
to changing times; ultimately, "The question of belief's ir-
relevant. " Caught in ambiguities in his final meditations,
Horatio reflects that in the "death of logic" he has "made my
peace/ With old illusion. " Plutzik has evidently undertaken
to make a universal myth of his sequel to Hamlet, exploiting
and drawing out the elements of self-examination and ambiguity which have always held modern appeal in the play, and
modifying Shakespearian blank verse for the modern ear. Intellectually appealing, touching brilliance as a commentary,
the poem has a growing emotional remoteness. Yet the narrative, though murky with intricacies of thought and overlays
of Greek, Christian and Freudian myth, has a decided interest
for Shakespeare devotees.   LJ

JULIA RANDALL

The Puritan Carpenter.   University of North Carolina Press,
1965, 80 pages.

      The craft and song are of a high technical order but
too frequently derivative--in a dozen poems patently of Yeats,
in "The Company" with literal attribution in his own accents
as he wrote: "And Yeats may dine at journey's end/ With
Landor and with Donne/ And all irascible scribbling men/ Who
put such passion on. " Some of the others are "A Windy Ker-
chief, " "Trim Reckoning, " "A Prayer for Parents Day"

("Some minister or saint/ Decried a sandy house"), "Cirque
d'Hiver." "Lurcher from Genesis, long man of light (For
T. R. ") summons up Dylan Thomas' sonnets. These and the
factitious speech of "Science and Poetry" would not be worth
emphasizing were it not for the poet's great skill. My own
preference is for two poems to Wordsworth, "from Virginia"
and "from Vermont, " the latter with its admonitory lines, "In
joy we start, / And grow by words apart. " (Allen Tate liked
this book very much, calling it "one of the few distinguished
volumes of the 1960's. ")   LJ

JOHN CROWE RANSOM

Selected Poems (Third Edition, Revised and Enlarged). Knopf,
1969, 159 pages.

Not very often can a poet live to establish the canon
of his own work, including the apocrypha and its exegesis too.
John Crowe Ransom at 81 did these things in the third
("final") edition of his Selected Poems--Revised and Enlarged.
      The third edition's principal interest, inasmuch as no
wholly new poem appears in it, lies in the final section called
"Sixteen Poems in Eight Pairings. "
      Here, like a self-indulgent, pedagogical host puttering
about his own house of verse, Ransom compares the "A"
(original) and "B" (revised) versions of eight poems. For
these pieces, which he classes as "deficient, " the poet passes
from textual notes on the "A" versions to discursive com-
mentaries on the "B" revisions.
      "Master's in the Garden Again, " for example, affords
the pleasure of overhearing a distinguished man of letters reflecting upon word play, idea, rhyme. In every instance,

though, the original version remains the purer form.

Ransom, a tutorial figure for the Southern "Fugitive Poets, " the New Criticism, and The Kenyon Review (which he founded), retired from teaching at Kenyon College two decades ago; his many honors include the Bollingen Prize and National Book Award for Poetry.   Recently he observed that "there has been no period in my life happier than this late one, where I am in the verse patch again. "

For all its genteel quality Ransom's verse is strongly fibred and has a definite spine.   His mannered, odd, precise style envelops archaisms--as Hardy's did--in what must be recognized as a permanent voice.

From this writer's "careful refining of the second edition" plus about 20 pieces more from earlier volumes, eight poems are surely candidates for the ultimate American anthology: "Bells for John Whiteside's Daughter, " "Piazza Piece, " "Blue Girls, " "Winter Remembered, " "The Equilibrists, " "Parting Without a Sequel, " "Captain Carpenter, " and "Prelude to an Evening. "

These are the first stanzas of "Winter Remembered":

Two evils, monstrous either one apart,
Possessed me, and were long and loath at going;
A cry of Absence, Absence, in the heart,
And in the wood the furious winter blowing.

Think not, when fire was bright upon my bricks,
And past the tight boards hardly a wind could enter,
I glowed like them, the simple burning sticks,
Far from my cause, my proper heat and center.

TIM REYNOLDS

Ryoanji.   Harcourt, 1964, 58 pages.

"Difficulties of a Birdhouse Builder, " Reynolds' colloquial
first piece, could just as well be printed as prose ("I do the
best I can. Still and all, though, " etc.). But selectivity and
concreteness refine the next--"What It Is Is"--also in syllabic
rather than metrical measure, to poetry. Picking up a pebble
the poet reflects that, "pounded/ on abrasive beaches, " now
"after ages' tumbling its chilly/ weight warms to my hand. "
He continues: "think, all this gravid dirt was stone!" and the
meanings of "gravid" (heavy, pregnant) sound together and recall the title poem about the Japanese Ryoanji Temple garden
of stones. A number of diversionary literary pieces include
a 17th century rhymed-couplet imitation and "Fragment of a
Homeric Hymn, " besides three sonnets after Ronsard, verses
after Horace and Breton, and the conventional blank verse of
"To a Bad Heart. " Reynolds' most ambitious inclusion,
"Hagiograph, " closes its last section, "The Rock": "In all
that reach of field/ only that rock is unplowed, unsown, and
will not yield--. " Under, "The Wave" receding, with physical weight "Boulders fought up through collapsed surf to
air. " The stones are the garden; and "Tombstones remain
after/ the marked life has gone to/ seed, / illegible. "
Adroit where it is derivative, and spare, objective, toughly
masculine where it is most the poet's own.   LJ

RUSSIAN POETRY

The Poets of Russia, 1890-1930, by Renato Poggioli. Harvard University Press, 1960, 383 pages.

Poggioli, professor of Slavic and Comparative Literature
and chairman of the Department of Comparative Literature at
Harvard, contributes to his discipline a panoramic and richly

detailed study of modern Russian poetry, from Brjusov's
Russian Symbolists in 1894 through Pasternak's collected
poems in 1933.   Starting with backgrounds (its 200-year span
makes Russian the "youngest major literature of the world"),
and then the age of Pushkin, he traces the work and fortunes
of Decadents and Symbolists, with side-studies of Western
trends and influences as well as the visual arts and theater.
He devotes a full chapter to Blok, "most highly creative figure
of his age, " representing a new culmination three-quarters of
a century after the great trio of Pushkin, Lermontov, and
Tjutchev.   The period 1910-1930 was dominated by the final
advance guard movements of Futurism (Majakowski) and Imag-
inism (Esenin) before Stalin assigned poets the role of "engi-
neers of the human soul"; and according to Pasternak, with
the period ending in Majakowski's suicide in 1930, "poetry
ceased to exist. "   (Poggioli calls Doctor Zhivago a "kind of
morality play, " its motif "the passive resistance of an in-
flexible soul. ")   This scholarly examination contains analyses
of many significant poems in its impressive coverage of an
area of growing interest.   In his foreword the author says it
is "as a foreigner that he handles the language he writes in";
but he comments elsewhere that the inborn virtues of Russian
are "assimilation" and "flexibility, " and the duality of his
language awareness seems to have added timbre and vitality
to generous scholarship.   LJ

NELLY SACHS

The Seeker and Other Poems, translated by Ruth and Matthew
Mead and Michael Hamburger.   Farrar, Straus & Giroux,
1970, 399 pages.

Nelly Sachs' entire family except for her mother were put to death in the Nazi gas chambers. The two survivors reached Norway in 1940 through the intercession of author Selma Lagerlof.

In 1966, at the age of 75, Nelly Sachs was named co-winner of the Nobel Prize for Literature.

Her "mangled music, " an "intense reaction to the Jewish spirit of suffering" became available to English readers when O the Chimneys appeared in 1967. That volume contained translations of about half her poetic output.

Published in 1970, the year of her death, The Seeker completes the English version of her poetry. Translated by Ruth and Matthew Mead and Michael Hamburger, all of whom participated in the 1967 work, this bilingual edition carries the German and English text on facing pages.

Lamentations or chants about the chosen people of God and sorrow, these poems point in many of their subjects and even the simplest signs toward the extermination camps:

> the soles of our shoes
> which stand like open graves at evening.

"Chorus of Clouds, " with its tutoring angels, recalls Rilke:

> We play at dying,
> accustom you gently to death.
> You, the inexperienced, who learn nothing in the nights.
> Many angels are given you
> but you do not see them.

Finally, in the section "Eclipse of the Stars, " Nelly Sachs foresees the death of our burnt-out planet:

> perhaps an eyeless place in the sky
> in which other constellations begin to shine
> drawn like bees by the scent of what has been--

Her restrained declamatory manner runs to invocation and refrain: "Golem death!"; "O Israel!"; "O my mother";

"O hear me. " Israel is apostrophized as "rememberer among
the nations" of things forgotten, "meteor-deep in the grave of
night. " And this poet names, recalls and installs in her
poems "the lost vocal chord at the room's empty throat, "
through images that rise from the unconscious. The recent
dead are remembered together with the archetypal David,
Ruth, Saul, Elijah, Rachel.

"Out of the Desert Sand" sounds a central theme--the
desert of apparent lifelessness, from which the creeds and
Israel sprang, or have come to rebirth. Affirmation, difficult and astringent, makes its way from the crematoria and
the victims, with never a direct mention of the killers, to
"What Darknesses": "Oh, no arrival without death. "

Poet of reconciliation, Nelly Sachs turns to her personal farewell: "Thus I ran out of the word"; "The color of
homecoming is always deep and dark. " And, from "A Sheaf
of Lightning":

> After this life's forgiveness
> out of the ravaged styles of writing
> out of the only second
> the inner ocean lifts
> its white crown of silence
> to you in eternal bliss--.

STEPHEN SANDY

Stresses in the Peaceable Kingdom.   Houghton Mifflin, 1967,
105 pages.

Stephen Sandy, raised in Minneapolis and a Harvard
English instructor, has gathered in his first volume 48 poems
written over eight years and published in such magazines as
The Atlantic, Poetry, and Contact.   They testify to a discern-
ing eye for particularity, sense of form, and irradiating

energy of composition.

Among the longer poems "Hiawatha, " with Minnehaha
Falls and the Hiawatha statue for theme and setting, will
surely ring a bell for all those who in their own childhood
played along the curtain of water Sandy describes:

> Then
> sun alone webbed our eyes; the misty
> light walked on our legs.
> We passed that sun-fired wall, boulder-
> heavy, heavy enough to drag a boy down
> in its scathing heave. . . .

Rightness of image flashes out everywhere in such descriptive and personal poems as "The Norway Spruce, "
"Wild Ducks, " "Light in Spring Poplars, " and in the "Grass-
hopper" seen hopping along on cement where it "snapped/ and
leapt, dodged gusts and spaces. "

In "Hunter's Moon, " "An airborne dragon-/ fly brash
with first frost/ buzzed me where I lay. " Or at the zoo the
poet considers "the matted locks of the lion. It is/ a bush
where dark, forgotten triumphs nest. . . . / The paw hovers/
tenderly, as if the whiskers were wounded. " In "The Wool-
worth Philodendron, " with perhaps a touch of Wallace Stevens,

> I have begun to see
> a careless wildness, long-leaved and green,
> mesh with dark plots implicit in the sun.

There are rather exotic poems about India and the East, appar-
ently known in service, and, very rarely, lines as prosy in
statement as in "Power Flows to Trouble" (the November 1965
Eastern states power failure): "When the lights went out/ we
did not know how/ big a failure we/ were part of. "

Sandy's uses of the ballad refrain are effective and
memorable. He adapts the traditional form to a tragedy of
today in "The Ballad of Mary Baldwin":

> The grass grows green, and roses red.
> Go do the dishes. Go to bed.

And in the refrain of "Breaks, " a simple poem about separation: "It is the time, the space between us, wins. "

MAY SARTON

A Durable Fire.   Norton, 1972, 80 pages.

   May Sarton's prologue poem, "Gestalt at Sixty, " states
the theme of A Durable Fire, most recent of her two dozen
books in verse and prose.   It sums up the latest year of her
decade spent "rooted in these (New Hampshire) hills" where
"Solitude exposes the nerve" and "the past, never at rest,
flows through it. "

> I am moving
> Toward a new freedom
> Born of detachment,
> And a sweeter grace--
> Learning to let go.

   The following poems form a kind of log that charts
Miss Sarton's spiritual temperature over the days and seasons
of that year as she looks back on one unhappy love and ex-
periences the tensions brought by another.   Book and year end
with her therapy and with a new and liberating attachment to
her psychiatrist, a woman, to whom the book is dedicated.

   Diaries arouse curiosity, and, read as a personal doc-
ument, A Durable Fire provokes this kind of interest.   As
poetry, carefully wrought, its conspicuous values are clarity
and precision in the perceptions of country things and of
emotions felt in solitude.   The poetry loses its balance and
weaves in and out of triteness through inordinate pursuit and
repetition of a preordained theme.   In "Autumn Sonnets" that
theme or resolution of the book, keyed by the prologue, sounds
again:

> Twice I have set my heart upon a sharing,
> Twice have imagined a real human home....
> I ponder it again and know for sure
> My life has asked not love but poetry.

May Sarton's lyrical predilections are suggested by the book's epigraph chosen from Sir Walter Raleigh, which contains her title, and by "Winter Carol, " an Elizabethan song ("Black mood, away!"). Further confirmation comes in the play on words of "The Snow Light, " a tone poem, and in a preference for the Shakespearian sonnet form. As a modern voice, however, she usually holds the rein on meter and employs a strict diction.

"Surfers" and other poems give analogies to the meeting and parting of lovers, items of the personal chronicle which deepens in the central "Autumn Sonnets":

> The phone became a monstrous instrument....
> Something got frayed of all we felt and meant.
> It was the year of testing.   Now we know
> Exactly what was asked: we had to grow.

This hackneyed recital continues into the conclusion which tells how "in this testing year beyond desire" the two "Began to move toward durable fire. "

Apart from May Sarton's principal concern there are poems about her parents, an elegy for Louise Bogan, and such personals as "Prisoner at a Desk. " All are thematic tributaries flowing toward the final section called "Letters to a Psychiatrist"--a functionary described as "This angel ... anarchic, fierce, full of laughter":

> Still the impersonal wing
> Does shelter, provides a place, a climate
> Where the soul can meet itself at last.

"Christmas Letter, 1970" and the final entries record the release and freedom attained through therapy, and the poet's acceptance of the solitary detachment which can foster creativity.

MAY SARTON

The Lion and the Rose.   Rinehart, 1948, 104 pages.

The opening poems of The Lion and the Rose--"Theme
and Variations, " written in New Mexico--attain a diction pure
and rare as the contemplated scene of desert and mountain.

high desolate
Lands where earth is skeleton.

In the last of these variations, "Difficult Scene, " the poet
suggests that the "implacable" and "austere" visual perspective provides a context in which one may achieve also a clear
spiritual perspective, "passion" may become "compassion. "
In this recognition, an act of resignation that is also conquest, the poet undergoes a transmutation of experience.
"Absence, " the transvaluated past, becomes "the greatest
Presence. "   This is also the theme of her title poem closing
the section.   Here the lion symbolizes past experience, "The
flaming lions of the flesh, " "All that is young and bold. " The
rose represents the final form of experience, the poet's arti-
fact, from absorption of these physical data into the "inward
sun" of spiritual re-creation.   And again the desired alchemy
requires resignation:

God of the empty room
Thy will be done. Thy will be done....
That in this death-in-life, delicate, cold,
The spiritual rose
Flower among the snows--

In the closing lines of the two poems occurs another restate-
ment; the "passion" become "compassion" of the first parallels "The love surpassing love" of the latter.

I have suggested a gloss to point up the symbolic
language, which carries a conviction of condensed experience
in these poems (May Sarton's best of the collection), because

later she abandons this method and the personal urgency which gives it tension. She goes outside her limited but exquisite technical range, and projects material that has not undergone alchemical translation.

The poems of part two, "American Landscapes," are perceptive evocations of place. A considerable vein of didacticism emerges, however (to re-emerge in later poems), as when, after being shown Monticello, "spacious, intimate and full of light," our expanding minds are abruptly deflated by this homily:

> The time must come when, from the people's heart,
> Government grows to meet the stature of a man,
> And freedom finds its form, that great unruly art,
> And the state is a house designed by Jefferson.

Certain other poems responding to the war do constitute a poetic summation of "our long tragic history"--for instance, "To the Living." The love poems possess a troubling beauty ("Night Storm," "Perspective"); in this immemorial preserve of lyric poets May Sarton is, to use her own phrase, "a delicate disturber of the soul." Again, the felicity of the opening poems appears in her portraiture of nature; she is perhaps above all a limner, and I believe that her least successful work comes when she strays outside the bounds of this gift, of the capacity to write,

> Now over everything the autumn light is thrown
> And every line is sharp, and every leaf is clear,
> Now without density or weight the airy sun
> Sits in the flaming boughs, an innocent fire...

Her last poem, "Celebrations," abandons the delicate craft in which her best verse is done for a free-cadenced categorical profession of faith in all "creators" who make for One World:

> For all creators everywhere in this time,
> For all those who design the forms of freedom in many ways,
> The statesman, teacher, poet, soldier, architect, mother--
> These are professions. The people involved in these professions

    Profess belief, move from faith, act to plan....
The awkward double play on "profess" emphasizes a general
slackness.   One cannot doubt May Sarton's genuine concern,
but she has moved beyond the terms of "the lion" and "the
rose, " outside the field of tension whose poles are so represented.   The need for social affirmation lacks the poetic
validity of that need for personal affirmation projected in
"Theme and Variations. "   Poetry

KARL SHAPIRO

The Bourgeois Poet.   Random, 1964, 120 pages.

    "Who are these that compound the mystery?   Tell me
about the Dewey Decimal system. "   The jacket observes that
in Trial of a Poet (1947) there are two examples of Shapiro's
new form "in which he eschews not only rhyme but versification as well. "   These poems are paragraphs, unified by
theme, or anti-proverbs, or (No. 64) guilt-ejecting Songs of
Myself.   They present a reversed Emerson, a Whitman hob-
bled by Ginsberg, an aphoristic Henry Miller.   One of the
urban roughs--"Of love and death in the Garrison State I
sing"; "If I don't take the wrong side, who will?"--Shapiro
catalogs city events, settings, feelings, and gives personal
anecdotes which are (as the title suggests) honest and self-
depreciating.   Of the coteries which he once "lawyer-style"
defended, Shapiro says, "The worshipers must be cured to
live in the world outside their arts.   Only then will the arts
flow freely.... "   That's right but is it art?   One trouble,
with the heightening largely left out, is that the response to
"Why must grown people listen to rhyme?" (for example) can
be just as downrightly "Why mustn't they?"   Or, why music?

And Shapiro's frequently used device of parallelism can be just as deadly as rhyme or metrical convention.   But all comment spent, the book holds unflagging interest.   LJ

KARL SHAPIRO

White-Haired Lover.   Random House, 1968, 37 pages.

These love poems, written for Teri, the young wife of the poet's middle age, go back in form to Karl Shapiro's early manner.   Nearly all lyrical, in traditional patterns, the 29 poems of White-Haired Lover mark a reversal from the prose paragraph style of The Bourgeois Poet (1964), which was an iconoclastic, frank confessional and contained the inquiry, "Why should grown people listen to rhyme?"

Rhymes are back with the difference that, in predominantly sonnet form, Shapiro continues to pursue the frank confessional vein.   This book is suffused, too, with the eroticism and the irreverence which showed up in the poet's free verse romp off the reservation.

A Romeo who can thumb his nose while saying his lines ("June of terrific promises and lawsuits"), he also writes with the clear beauty of "After the Storm":

> The diamond morning walks on broken glass,
> Or is it tears we see through in our kiss
> After the wreckage of the night that has
> Unblinded us and stripped the ponderous trees.
> I love you and I fall upon my knees
> And gather you like heavens of sweet grass.

Readers who have followed Shapiro's progress from V-Letter, which spoke for the World War II GI, on through his defense of "literary coteries" and into the somersault position represented by his essays In Defense of Ignorance, will be interested but not surprised to read him in his newest incarnation.

Some of these love poems move the emotions less than they exercise the curiosity as they chronicle pains and delights, ups and downs, of a late-blooming rǫmance. They do not add to the poet's reputation, ratified by his sharing the 1969 Bollingen Award with John Berryman, for his Selected Poems. But they do show that Karl Shapiro has lost none of his assurance and ease with conventional verse.

MARY SHUMWAY

Song of the Archer and Other Poems. Regnery, 1964, 64 pages.

The title poem clusters images about a country girlhood with its central event, the grandmother's death. From the verbal shock of such imagery as "Light spattered in pulsing garnets on the sand. The river slugged east/ Clotting above the dam, " free rhythms relax to redolent ease: "Flocks on the summerwood danced in the wine/ Of quiet blossoms, where sweet owls called a/ Comforting wide night. " Mary Shumway, a Californian, has for her long lead poem's theme the transformation of experience into art, a theme emphasized by refrains taken from Yeats' "Sailing to Byzantium. " Among the other poems, "I Have Walked Ginger Among Those Pungent Leaves" has a touch of Dylan Thomas, and "the wounded/ finch healed heaven with its cries, " of Blake; but Miss Shumway's poetry is deeply feminine and personal, with intimate small rains and "Teacups of Love. " (Cup imagery appears also in "Windcups Swinging, " "cup of light, " "cup of his hands. ") This lovely, reverent voice returns in the last poem, "On Mt. Tamalpais, " to the life-art translation theme: "after the sun/ Has set, the rare perception fails, / the metaphor endures. "   LJ

ELI SIEGEL

Hail, American Development.   Definition Press, 1968, 194
pages.

Siegel seems to describe his own school of Aesthetic
Realism in one of his notes, "The Poems Looked At": "The
particularity of sound is separation; the relation of sound is
junction.   When, in sound, we hear separation and junction,
at once, we ... hear music." The notes really are an ad-
junct poetry, occupying 65 pages and continuing the obsession
with temporal juxtapositions, endless permutations of facts
and words.   In a decorous vernacular free verse, Siegel ex-
horts (against the Vietnamese war); fixes moments in time
("What Now Coheres of 1861-1865?"); introduces "found" poems
(a passage in Kant arranged as verse); translates Baudelaire,
Verlaine, Catullus. Omnivorous ("This seen now: a fly"), un-
dauntedly idiosyncratic.   LJ

ALAN SILLITOE

Love in the Environs of Voronezh.   Doubleday, 1969, 63
pages.

Alan Sillitoe is an Englishman known best for his fiction about English working class life, notably Saturday Night
and Sunday Morning and The Loneliness of the Long Distance
Runner.

The poems of his third collection of verse are tough,
terse, often opaque.   The title piece, "Love in the Environs
of Voronezh, " closing the volume, concerns a Russian town
smashed by war, "Yet love rebuilt it street by street." Like
a cordon of bone the war dead ring the reborn city.   For

them but also for the survivors

> There's no returning to the heart:
> The dead to the environs go
> Away from resurrected stone.

Sillitoe's lyrical shorthand never expands to become fullthroated or more than sparing with imagery. His themes include love, travel, Russia and the endurance of her people, the experience of writing.

"Siberian Lake, " the most fused and striking poem here, typifies an invariably somber mood and expressionist method:

> Black ice smoulders all around. Dusk
> Approaches without sound or reason.
> Water below moves its shoulders
> Like a giant craving to see snow.

"Ditchling Beacon, " written as from inside the observed event, describes a shot bird, "Feathers dipping toward oaken frost. " Images of loneliness and destruction and a tone of barely muted anxiety haunt all the poems, hard-earned, insular as they seem. For example there is "Window" with its "They call it love/ A vicious loneliness. " Or the ironic "Made for Each Other. " "End" provides a bone-simple epitaph for an epoch of violence:

> Bullet, bomb
> Arm off, head gone
> Hole is, limb black
> Where sun shone.

A "Midwestern Missile Man" addresses God as his rocket climbs, "The foaming jackpot climbing high" to "Obliterate your magic eye. " Other titles--"Ride It Out, " "Survival, " "Suicide"--insist on man's lot in an inhuman and godforsaken existence.

These are poems of a writer who does not believe that words can exorcise and doubts that they can bless. For him they express the last pride of intent to endure. "First Poem"

with its hard cry, hanging tough, might be taken as Sillitoe's
credo:

> Burned out, burned out.
> Water of rivers hold me
> On a course toward sea.

EDITH SITWELL

Music and Ceremonies.   Vanguard, 1963, 44 pages.

"Poetry is indeed the deification of reality, " Dame
Edith writes in her preface.   This aim, accomplished here
through a ritual language rich in texture and rhythm, rebukes
what she calls "a general attempt on the part of incompetent
versifiers to remove all grandeur from poetry. "   "The War
Orphans" typically combines a subject of deep human concern
and personal sympathy with splendor of expression.   "At the
Crossroads" delights with sheer sensuous sound: "In the
month of mellow August, of the auguries/ Of dust, and yellow
moons and melons ... "   A personal note resounds within the
tradition of English eloquence: "I, an old dying woman, tied/
To the winter's hopelessness/ And to a wisp of bone" ("His
Blood Colors My Cheek").   The title poem with its frequent
imagery of spring storm concludes the collection: "Music and
Ceremonies keep/ Green heaven high in air and the green
earth/ Beneath our dancing feet.... "   This book of fourteen
pieces written since Edith Sitwell's Collected Poems (1954)
belongs beside it.   LJ

PAUL JORDAN SMITH (editor)

Poetry from Hidden Springs.   Doubleday, 1962, 232 pages.

An anthology of verse by eighty "nonprofessional and occasional poets" from Bruno to Havelock Ellis, this unaccountably includes a long selection from the marathon sonneteer Merrill Moore, and poems by Melville and Joyce. Not only is the selective principle doubtful, but few of the "happy surprises" promised by the rather moralistic and prescriptive introduction occur. Two inclusions recall the graceful, half-forgotten April Twilights (1923) by Willa Cather. Most of the verse is form-bound, conventional, and adds up to an ineffective counterattack upon "modern" poetry despite the editor's clear intent.   LJ

W. D. SNODGRASS

After Experience. Harper & Row, 1968, 92 pages.

After Experience records fluently and compulsively the history of personal loss and estrangement begun in the author's Heart's Needle (1959), which won the Pulitzer Prize. Some of it comes almost raw:

> Before we drained out one another's force
> With lies, self-denial, unspoken regret
> And the sick eyes that blame; before the divorce
> And the treachery. Say it: before we met.

Following the personal poems are five about paintings, most of which seem like a dogged virtuoso extension of Auden's "Musée des Beaux Arts"--for example, the four-page "Manet: The Execution of the Emperor Maximilian." The remarkable exception, "Van Gogh: The Starry Night, " anatomizes and dissects that painting with a scalpel of light. Interspersing quotes from the artist, Snodgrass transmutes passion into compassion as he does not in the songs made from his own sorrow.

The poet, who has entered into "The Starry Night, " imagines there are small steady commonplaces:

Between the houses, fruit trees, or narrow
Lanes beneath the eaves-troughs and the dark
Shrubs; in back, laid out side by side
The kitchen gardens with their heavy odors
Where dew sits chilly on the cabbage leaves.

The last quarter of the book contains translations, most from Rilke but including also Rimbaud, Yves Bonnefoy and others.

Contained in conventional precise forms, the theme of personal loss in the first section establishes a pervasive tone carrying into "A Flat One" about the horror of protracted dying: "Pain was your only occupation. " "Pow-wow" continues the lamentation: "like a woman nursing a sick child she already knows will die. "

Social satire breaks out sometimes, as in "Leaving Ithaca": "They go for the main chance/ But always save the weekend for their passions;/ They dress just far enough behind the fashions/ And think right thoughts. "

W. D. Snodgrass searches his wounds and those of others with skin-crawling detachment. Under the decorum of the strict stanzas, the urbane versification, lie a horror of complacent existence and "the heart of an immense darkness."

HY SOBILOFF

Breathing of First Things.   Dial, 1963, 125 pages.

"The Quest for the Child Within, " title of James Wright's introduction, gives the general theme. With free sensory freshness Sobiloff writes in "Speak to Me Child" (a phrase itself used over and over): "Promise me child before

you disappear in hide-and-seek/ That your next step will be
the fiction of this world/ That when you leave the broken
wall/ You will keep your lizard spontaneities. " There is a
range from the childlike rhyme-as-you-go of "Between
Flights..." to the complicated language of "Who Will I Be
like"; always the instantaneous as if given instantly by a child;
deceptively casual verbal compression with verbs and nouns
descriptive ("The White Moon": "I saw a man on country
horseback/ A field asleep with half-sized cows"). "You
Cannot Paint Nature" sets against innocence (desired overall)
the world's essential inscrutability, sea-depths "Where the
soundings unknown do not listen. " Except for four reprinted
from earlier volumes, all poems in this extensive collection
are new in book form, though a number have appeared in
literary reviews and anthologies.   LJ

WOLE SOYINKA

A Shuttle in the Crypt. Hill and Wang, 1972, 89 pages.

        The spirit of black Africa wears a costume of Western
culture in these prison poems by Wole Soyinka, Nigerian
playwright and poet. Soyinka was imprisoned in Nigeria from
1967 to 1969 for giving support to secessionist Biafra. He
has since resumed his old position as director of the Drama
School at the University of Ibadan.
        The language of these poems is ultra-literary, with
reflections upon Hamlet, Gulliver, Ulysses; it is studded as
well with poetic archaisms such as "'tis" and inversions such
as "Responsive ever. "
        The "negritude" of the poems is not on the formal
surface but in an opulence, a fecundity of rhythmic images

too slippery sometimes to grasp in their passage. It's difficult to image how much of A Shuttle in the Crypt could indeed
have been written down "in the dark or during a moment of
slackened surveillance, " full as many of the poems are and
deprived as Soyinka was of writing material.

He records that it was the poems' composition, filling
and directing his subjective experience, which kept him sane
while imprisoned. The poet became the secretive shuttle of
his title, "a trapped weaverbird" within his solitary prison.
The verse "Prisonettes" worked to let out rage, and he
achieved self-hypnosis in the "mental pacing" of the poems'
repetitions.

The imprisoned poet turned to Hindu metaphysics for
his "Recession":

>   a song of cyclones in silence of shells
>   the dew departing to primacy of waters.

He explains "Mahapralaya, " the Hindu concept provid-
ing his theme, as "the return of the universe to its womb...
the consoling experience of man in the moment of death, the
freeing of his being from the death of the world. "

In such capacity for transcendence came Soyinka's victory over his prison cell. He refers to his book as "a map
of the course trodden by the mind, " the road on which he
balanced rage and forgiveness.

Often the poems seem filled with unweeded verbiage,
and clotted lines knot up the poet's meaning. There's a deluge
of imagery associated with death and rebirth, usually biblical
and with Lazarus for archetype. The execution of five pri-
soners brings to a poem the grim football-like refrain, "Tread
Drop Dead Drop Dead. "

But a bitter humor enters "Live Burial" with "Lest it
rust / We kindly borrowed his poetic license. " And "Future

Plans" can pun: "The meeting is called to odium. " The
"Epilogue, " dedicated to George Jackson and others, expresses
both beauty and courage:

> Not that he loved sunrise less
> But truly, as love's caress
> Whose craving must to spring devices lead.

SPECTRA

The Spectra Hoax, by William Jay Smith.   Wesleyan University Press, 1961, 158 pages.

This is the first full account of "Spectra"--that ambitious, delightful and successful literary hoax of 1916-18--and
its creators, Emanuel Morgan (Witter Bynner) and Anne Knish
(Arthur Davison Ficke).   Their spoof took in Poetry and
Others, critics, fellow poets Masters, W. C. Williams and
Kreymborg, and ended by almost taking in the perpetrators
themselves and modifying their styles.   In the preface to the
1916 volume, republished here in full, Anne Knish analyzed
Spectrism: "Just as the colors of the rainbow recombine into
a white light" so "The rays which the poet has dissociated
into colorful beauty should recombine in the reader's brain
into a new intensity.... " Typical of Knish-Ficke's free-verse
dissociations, this about a wakened sleeper: "I will not con-
sort with reformed corpses. " Bynner's role was free-rein
rhyming, a burlesk of novelty cults.   The two masterminded
their plot at Fiske's Davenport, Iowa, home, and in deference
to their wives carried it out across the river in a Moline
hotel with the help of Scotch.   The poets abetted themselves
in reviews and lectures, and finally introduced a third part-
ner, Marjorie Allen Seiffert, as Elijah Hay.   In the author's
words, "Spectra is a tonic reminder that it is always both

helpful and healthful to laugh. "   LJ

GEORGE STARBUCK

Bone Thoughts. Yale University Press, 1960, 58 pages.

        The first volume of an accomplished poet whose themes
are love, war, and the spiritual temper of the times.   Boston, where Starbuck has lived, provides much of the setting
for some rich composition: "Spring, like an ill bird, settles
to the masthead/ of here and there an elm.   The streets are
misted. /   A Boston rain, archaic and monastic, / cobbles the
blacktop waters. . . . "   Technically adroit, at one moment in
"Poems from a First Year in Boston" he becomes a jivy
Hopkins ("And the bride's/ the broad's the broodmare's Moon
at a cloud's side/ poses"), and another, a Robert Lowell:
"Jonathan Edwards, did you stop off here/ where marsh birds
skittered, and a longboat put/ its weed-grown bones to pasture at the foot/ of Beacon, close on Charles Street?" But
mostly the verse is sparer and makes an easy conciliation
between traditional prosody and modern speech.   "Elegy" concludes: "the world is wide God knows, but sex is deep: pull
your dashboards tight about your necks and sleep. " Light
verse disarmingly bears the serious intent of poems such as
"Prognosis": "the insecure/ vaccinate themselves--with fear."
Dudley Fitts' introduction is short and serviceable.   LJ

WALLACE STEVENS (about)

The Act of the Mind: Essays on the Poetry of Wallace
Stevens, Roy Harvey Pearce and J. Hillis Miller, eds.
Johns Hopkins Press, 1965, 304 pages.

Wallace Stevens' Collected Poems of 1955, the year of
his death, closed with "Not Ideas About the Thing but the
Thing Itself. " The title evinces his absorption in a "com-
presence" of Reality and Imagination.   Latest of his winter
pieces, its frugality and suppressed splendor reveal Stevens'
effort to match style with the fluidity of experience.   The Act
of the Mind pivots on this late style from which the earlier
rhetorical flair and gaudiness ("The Comedian as the Letter
C") have been purged.   Titles of the eleven essays (all but
four published in English Literary History) specify their concerns among the expanding Stevens explication and criticism
and impulse to fix a canon.   Among them are Samuel French
Morse, "WS, Bergson, Pater"; J. Hillis Miller, "WS' Poetry
of Being" ("Thinkers without final thoughts/ In an always in-
cipient cosmos"); Helen Hennessy Vendler, "The Qualified
Assertions of WS"; Marc Hammond, "On the Grammar of WS"
("Poetry about poetry [metapoetry] is the key phrase... ");
Joseph N. Riddel, "The Contours of Stevens Criticism" (he
had "weathered three decades of Eliot's broadsides against
romanticism" and created "a new secular [and humanistic]
poetry"; an American modern, he confronted "the diminished
dignity of poetry").   LJ

WALLACE STEVENS (about)

Stevens' Poetry of Thought, by Frank Doggett.   Johns Hopkins Press, 1966, 223 pages.

"The planet on the table, " Stevens called his poetry.
He held that simple concepts ("by concept he seems to mean
an idea married to an image") are the seedbed both of poetry
and philosophy.   Marking correspondences with Schopenhauer,

James, Bergson, Jung, Whitehead, Santayana, the author
warns against assuming a body of doctrine in the poems. In
Stevens' achievement, growing in critical estimation, "abstraction again becomes a major element in poetry"--contrary
to the edicts of Pound and Eliot. Doggett points up his "austere and candid agnosticism" (typically in "Esthétique du Mal"
Stevens protests "The genius of the body, which is our
world, / Spent in the false engagements of the mind"), and
in "Martial Cadenza" the tantalizing late intuition of an es-
sence "undated and eternal. " Chapter VI, "This Invented
World, " was included in The Act of the Mind (Stevens essays,
edited by R. H. Pearce and J. H. Miller, Johns Hopkins
Press, 1965). The chapter contains such useful clues as this
from Vaihinger, Nietzsche's Will to Illusion: "The World of
Being is an invention--there is only a world of Becoming...."
Other chapters discuss Stevens' concept of flux, the major
symbols and their philosophical implications.   LJ

DYLAN THOMAS   (about)

A Garland for Dylan Thomas, gathered & with preface by
George J. Firmage.   Clarke & Way, 1963, 171 pages.

This "garland" was gathered for the tenth anniversary
of Dylan Thomas' death on November 9, 1953--84 poems by
78 writers: a selected tribute from an unparalleled outpouring.
Frequent disclaimers, as in Lloyd Frankenberg's "A Refusal
To Mourn, Etc. " ("Everyone owns a share in you. / If it's
a he, he'll air a new Gospel of thick-as-thieves"), are followed hard by claimant reminiscences ("Once on a snarling
boulevard, / ...you gripped my arm"; or Ralph Pomeroy's
flat "And once he smiled at me beerily in a bar").   Among

the simply good is Ruthven Todd's "Laugharne Churchyard in
1954"; among the complex good is Isabella Gardner's "When
a Warlock Dies. " Numerous and dubious are such tributes by
imitation as Jean Garrigue's "A Mourning" ("When he paced
the shift of the sea cold side") and Burns Singer's hybrids
("scare-man-crow"). Jack Lindsay and Kenneth Rexroth write
in political anger, Rexroth's "Thou Shalt Not Kill" being the
strongest inclusion. It's pat but true to add that most absorb-
ing reading in the volume is Thomas' own "Notes on the Art
of Poetry, " written out in 1951 to answer five questions
asked by a student: "I read indiscriminately, and with my
eyes hanging out. I could never have dreamt that there were
such goings-on in the world between the covers of books, such
sand-storms and ice-blasts of words, such slashing of humbug, and humbug too, such staggering peace.... "   LJ

DYLAN THOMAS   (about)

The Religious Sonnets of Dylan Thomas: a Study in Imagery
and Meaning, by H. H. Kleinman. University of California
Press, 1963, 153 pages.

        Ten congested sonnets written by Dylan Thomas at the
age of 21 here receive earnest, exhaustive textual explication
by Mr. Kleinman, an associate professor of literature at the
Julliard School of Music. The reader probably will assent to
David Daiches' opinion that the poems are "altogether too
closely packed, too dense, to come across effectively. " But
specialist and devotee can admire the author's ransacking of
symbols for likely meaning and derivation and of literature
for suggestive parallels. These draw into consideration 17th-
century sermons, Blake, Milton, mandrake lore, Westerns,

Egyptian funerary customs, and much more.   The sonnets
move "from the Incarnation through the Crucifixion to an
apocalyptic prophecy. "   From the first, mocking "descent of
the Word, " to the climactic eighth, in which the Passion is
recorded as if by a shifting camera and voices, awe, punning,
ribaldry are mixed.   The ninth is set down as telescoping the
vegetation rite myths concerning burial and resurrection of
the god from Sir James Frazer.   (At first, says the expli-
cator, it "seems to be composed of fourteen lines of hier-
oglyphic verse to which even the Rosetta stone is no key. ")
But the final lines "ring plangently of the green garden and
the everlasting mercy. "   The reader is handicapped by omis-
sion of the text to which, a chapter for each sonnet, the book
is devoted--an inconvenience both because of Thomas' extreme
allusiveness and Kleinman's shorthand manner of exegesis. LJ

RUTHVEN TODD

Garland for the Winter Solstice.   Little, 1962, 160 pages.

        This is poetry of nature and man in nature, without
sweat and strain, collected from twenty-five years' output by
the Edinburgh-born English poet (resident in the United States
in Martha's Vineyard).   W. H. Auden thought of Todd as "a
Nineteenth Century Country Clergyman who has mysteriously
managed to get born and to survive in this hectic age. "   Some
of the poems, like "Max Ernst" and the sonnet "Paul Klee, "
seem to owe much to Auden, though they have individual force,
and Wilfred Owen can be detected among Todd's technical an-
cestors in poetry that communicates.   LJ

GEORG TRAKL

Twenty Poems of Georg Trakl, selected and translated by
James Wright and Robert Bly.   The Sixties Press, 1961, 61
pages.

A cluster of poetic perceptions, ripened in silence,
by a young German poet (he died at 27) of whom Rilke said:
"Trakl's poetry is to me an object of sublime existence...."
Sixties editor Robert Bly beautifully said of these sensitive
impersonal notations: "The silence is the silence of things
that could speak, but choose not to. "   The selection was made
from Trakl's Die Dichtungen (his later poems), one of three
collected volumes published in Salzburg by Otto Muller Ver-
lag.   In bilingual text on facing pages, there are such titles
as "Summer, " "On the Marshy Pasture, " and "The Evening":
"You shadows swallowed by the moon/   Sighing upward in the
empty goblet/   Of the mountain lake. "   LJ

LOUIS UNTERMEYER

Labyrinth of Love.   Simon & Schuster, 1965, 59 pages.

This little book of love lyrics has been freely de-
rived from one with the same title by Otto Bierbaum, a minor
nineteenth-century German poet whose verses were used by
Richard Strauss and other composers.   In his "Foreword for
H. L. Mencken"--who asked that he translate Bierbaum some
forty years earlier--Untermeyer comments: "Nostalgically
re-creating a set of period pieces, I ransacked Bierbaum's
poetic properties; I stole his title; I rearranged his sequence
and wrote new poems to suggest a contemporary love relationship. " An attractively bound and illustrated bibelot.   LJ

CESAR VALLEJO

Twenty Poems of Cesar Vallejo, chosen and translated by
John Knoepfle, James Wright and Robert Bly.   The Sixties
Press, 1963, 63 pages.

        James Wright, in his note on Vallejo, says: "Cur-
rent poets in the United States seem to be perishing on either
side of a grey division between century-old British formalism
on the one hand and a vandalism of anti-poetry on the other."
This bilingual volume is part of The Sixties Press program
of redress through introducing important foreign poets outside
the English tradition.   Vallejo, a Peruvian, died in 1938 (in
Paris) at 45.   He wrote of his family, of cold and hunger and
against fascism, in an oral Andean manner with folk-plaint
refrain.   There are surreal and vernacular elements in his
direct somber voice.   "Black Stone Lying on a White Stone"
closes: "These are the witnesses:/ the Thursdays, and the
bones of my shoulders, / the solitude, and the rain, and the
roads. . . . "   LJ

MARK VAN DOREN

That Shining Place.   Hill and Wang, 1969, 81 pages.

        That Shining Place gathers poems written since 1963,
the year Mark Van Doren's collected verse appeared; it was
published on the poet's 75th birthday.   The new lyrics continue
the pastoral tradition this poet shares pre-eminently with
Robert Frost.   Less substantial than the latter's, with a
thinner music, they are true notes of nature, the simplicities
of retirement to Connecticut life on a farm and the nostalgic
reflections of old age.

Frequently a refrain sounds its bell-like fading cadences:

> So fair a world it was,
> So far away in the dark, the dark,
> Yet lighted, oh, so well, so well:
> Water and land,
> So clear, so sweet;
> So fair, it should have been forever.

Many of the poems are in dialogue form, or suggest dialogue
--with the poet's wife, or perhaps with a youngster as in
"Wait Till Then":

> "A dull day. "
> "And yet it is a day. "
> "What else? What could it be?"
> "Why, nothing. "
> "Oh. "
> "You still don't understand, my child.
> A dark day is so much more than no day--"

Mark Van Doren taught English at Columbia from
1920 until he retired in 1959. His only comment on the social
scene here is that of a longtime teacher in "No More Build-
ings, " a piece about campus violence. However, the poem is
without bitterness and takes the form once again of dialogue.

Van Doren fends off "Old Age Blues" with celebrations of birds in the morning, a warming stove, spring shoots,
"Winter Calligraphy, " the first letter from a grandson ("All
capitals, and how they dance"), expostulations to an impassive
cat ("No, no, not birds.... Not chickadees--God!". New
England tradition dominates three poems, including one to John
Bradford, builder of the Cornwall, Connecticut, house in which
the Van Dorens lived. The book closes with eleven "Psalms"
that mingle Biblical cadences with a reverent modern speaking
voice.

No poem in the book is more attractive than "This
Man, " written "for Archibald MacLeish at 75":

Nobody, I think, will be there when he comes,
And coming, still walks on, his back so straight,
His voice so beautiful before him, sounding
The unknown dark. O love, O light,
Be with this man forever, be the gifts
That if I had them I would give to him
Who has no need of either love or light,
Being already blessed, this blazing man.

FRANÇOIS VILLON

The Complete Works of François Villon, translated by Anthony
Bonner. McKay, 1960, 228 pages.

      Anthony Bonner's Villon contains, after a foreword
by William Carlos Williams, a biography of the elusive medieval poet by the translator, all the vivid and frequently bawdy
poems known to have been written by him (Williams says
about 3000 lines) including two possibles, and a sizable body
of notes together with a selective bibliography and indexes of
first lines (in French), and of titles (in English). Bilingual
text on facing pages gives medieval French with unrhymed
colloquial rendition by Bonner. His free, direct translation
uses modern slang where necessary for truth of tone. Arrangement is in four sections: the two long works "The
Legacy" and "The Testament, " "The Miscellaneous Poems, "
and "The Poems in Slang. " Some of the ballades of course
stand alone, like that most famous one "of the Ladies of Bygone Times" with its refrain "Mais ou sont les neiges d'antan
(But where are the snows of bygone years)?" The longer
poems are studded with allusions which would be lost except
for the notes, but which with their help lead the reader into
the vanished atmosphere of Villon's Paris.   LJ

DAVID WAGONER

The Nesting Ground.   Indiana University Press, 1963, 64 pages.

In the title poem, killdeer lead curious viewers away
from the nestlings, and from a distance they watch "The
young spring out of cover, / Piping one death was over. "
People come in for ironic or tender musing in "Closing Time,"
"After Consulting My Yellow Pages, " and "Elegy for Simon
Corl, Botanist": "His door leaned open to the flies, / And
May, like tendrils, wandered in. " "Free Passage" brings a
contrasting freewheeling verse, inventive whirling words: "Oh
my snifter, my tumble-rick, sweet crank of the stars.... "
Wagoner's style, graphic and understated, mostly leaves his
sketches alone to have their say.   LJ

THEODORE WEISS

The World Before Us.   Macmillan, 1970, 287 pages.

Theodore Weiss, Princeton professor, editor, and
critic, selected the poems for this volume from his output
over two decades.   The World Before Us contains 55 poems
from four previous books together with 23 new ones--too dense
a company in view of his compressed and parenthetical style.
Lifelong, Weiss has written literally academic verse
abounding in discursive indirections and elaborations along
with his distinct graces of restrained music and fastidious diction.   A self-commentary occurs in "Studying French, " which
compares the poet's difficulty in that language with facility in
his own,

> my easy hold
> on everything, and everything.
> I who debonairly strolled (I rallied them,
> I twitted them
> with double talk) among my words.

It's in keeping that the themes should often be literary. "The Fire at Alexandria" imagines incineration of a complete Sophocles, of Homer's journals, and "magnificent authors kept in scholarly rows/ whose names we have no passing record of" lost.

One of Weiss' long poems, "Caliban Remembers," is a quasi-Shakespearian tour-de-force. Caliban now alone recovers the "drowned book" of The Tempest and dreams of changing places with Prospero, but at last decides he would give up the imagined power in exchange for his own "night air, free now, full of nothing but its own voice." Yet he longs "to hear once more those me-compelling voices."

Some poems with their obstinate, involved prolixity are not likely to hold any but equally obstinate and verse-adept readers. "Into Summer" misfires with an awkward analogy between the classroom and a burned-over field. "The Wine-Skin Foot," on the other hand, turning to the literary and classical allusion, restores the poet's fluent grace:

> And here, the dusk
> wine-spilt on the hills, the stars
> as they leaned on these pillars once,
> near for the centuries ago
> they first began, in twinkling airs
> repeat their haunting names again.

At his best again in "The Visit" Weiss writes of "this learned light now, ripening/ through autumn, as though the mellowing/ earth had finally imprinted itself/ a gloss, upon the quiet air."

The World Before Us sums up the poetic effort of a connoisseur of language and a scholar of cultural history. He feels compelled to write in "A Working Day": "We think, incredulously, of our first glossy/ learning, our pride: not one of the past, / the great we assumed we could lean on/ forever, has a word for this." Yet he quotes with approval Norbert Wiener's remark that "Man is the ultimate antientropy," and his testamentary poem "A Letter from the Pygmies" sounds his own final note of affirmation:

> In short, though there's a scheme
> afoot to blow Your ark and all in it
> to smithereens, to pitch a cloudy,
> climbing tower will convert the earth
> into one tomb, I know by feelings
> craning, preening deep inside
> the ark's still riding, riding high.

REED WHITTEMORE

Fifty Poems Fifty. University of Minnesota Press, 1970, 67 pages.

Among his confessional generation, Reed Whittemore can be tagged not just by the pervasiveness of his ironic wit but also by his willingness to inject himself with it.

He satirizes the egocentricity of such peers as Lowell, Berryman, and Shapiro in "A Fascinating Poet's Diary":

My impacted wisdom teeth are fascinating.
My diet, my sex life, my career, these also are fascinating.

Preference for restraint and a formal decorum characterize Whittemore as they do the satirists of prose. He is a personal essayist, his subjects drawn from the less-noticed corners of existence and the mind. They possess such minimal topicality as the sag in social tempo between political administrations in Washington, D. C. Or there is "Philanthropist," a melancholy humorous footnote on giving

("He draws two gravely wounded bucks from his sad wallet").

Intellectually cranky, this poet is most serious when
he appears most comical. He reveals at times, as through
the interstices of routine, the implacable mystery surrounding
our existence:

Who has the dream denied has the terror privilege....
In spring into the world slips a we, but slithers
In autumn softly away as furnaces wake
To their hopeless war against cold-and-forever.

"Osprey Sonnet" develops the writer's own variation
on the classic form. His theme here is "Having it made, "
sitting about in his own cave together with his mate; "rations
we had, and lore. "

A kind of reverse irony operates because of too seri-
ous a nonseriousness in the mytho-poem called "The Sick
Ones. " Running nine pages, it brings to mind Berryman's
Dream Songs in its argument and cryptic references.

The book's title, Fifty Poems Fifty, alludes to Whittemore's age at writing it as well as the number of pieces
included. So does "The Mind":

I know a mind, soul, whose time now leads it
Shoreward to silence.
Not long ago it chattered like half a school,
And bade the desert dance.

Whittemore's last previous volume, Poems, New and
Selected, was published in 1967. Once editor of both Furioso
and the Carleton Miscellany in Minnesota, he is now an English professor at the University of Maryland.

Reed Whittemore's verse essays carry most memorable force when they "dig the scene. " "Prayer, " with its
barely passing pun, "let freedom sting, " includes the line:
"Bear the loaf and fish to Xerox and press the black button."
"The Trouble Outside" expresses a sense of quiet involvement
as it instances the public library to contrast inner order with

outer turbulence:

> Yet it is outside the uptown branch that the inside has died. . . .
> The leaves are not in order, and not on file; nor the faces. . . .

These poems flash dexterity and wit. They are the poems of a mature questioner of our prized assurances and the typical American day.

REED WHITTEMORE

Poems: New and Selected.   University of Minnesota Press, 1967, 116 pages.

Reed Whittemore, for a long time professor of English at Carleton College where he was founding editor of that thorn on the academic rosebush, The Carleton Miscellany, has assembled a selection from his poems of twenty years, including five previous volumes. He is now on the staff of the National Institute of Public Affairs and a lecturer at Princeton.

Many drawn from his professional life, these are well-crafted reminiscent poems, a kind of familiar essay in verse.   There are occasional mood pieces such as the excellently sustained "On a Summer Sunday, " which closes:

> And that day,
> That somnolent summer Sunday day,
> Crept away, crept away
> To deep but delicate distances, as the den
> And the wood and the mind unobtrusively darkened,
> And the birds and the children slept, and the doors were still.

Many readers can relive old times through "Summer Concert" or "The Elm City, " with its recapture of streetcar times: "The hard, yellow, reversible, wicker seats/ Sit in my mind's warm eye, varnished row on row. . . . / I still hear the dishpan bell of the yellow trolley. "

However, seen together, so many concerned with

academic life and writers' conferences, the poems register
overall a deprecatory, minifying note. "Dear God" is typical:
"... to turn the eyes back in boredom to the more or less
boring self. " "Return, Alpheus (a Poem for the Elders of
Phi Beta Kappa)" repeats the burden:

> ... the muses are dead;
> In their stead
> Are only latticed sections of bored sky.

The most satisfying section probably is "Six Shaggy, "
seemingly inspired by John Berryman's "Dream Songs, " with
inversions, short-circuited locutions, and a sense of social
argument, as here:

> Once upon what time would loyal U. S. A. boy
> Be Commie?
> If boy said loyal bomb kill "peaceful citizen, "
> That's when....
> Rule 1: all U. S. soldier: boy.
> Rule 2: no boy Hanoi.

At his best as an occasional poet, Whittemore ap-
parently takes to heart his responsibilities as teacher and
poet in our world of which Loren Eiseley said: "We do not
like mists in this era, and the word imagination is less and
less used. " Yet it's as if that world sometimes reached
through an open window and restrained his pen from the joy
and abandon of a true song of himself.

JAMES WRIGHT

The Branch Will Not Break.   Wesleyan University Press,
1963, 59 pages.

Ware with words, James Wright in these poems ap-
prehends native scenes through alert perceptions, as in
"Autumn Begins in Martins Ferry, Ohio" or "To the Evening
Star, Central Minnesota": "Miles off, a whole grove silently/

Flies up into the darkness. /   One light comes on in the sky, /
One lamp on the prairie. "   The apprehending holds surrealist
infusions ("Beautiful daylight of the body, your hands carry
seashells"), and details have the exactness of oriental poems,
unified by mood.   American meditations carry retrospective
anguish and wonder ("Stages on a Journey Westward"; and
"Twilights":   "My grandmother's face is a small maple leaf /
Pressed in a secret box").   They set out to reclaim that experience at the tip of the senses.   Or there's awareness with
delight, the bluejay of "Two Hangovers":   "for he knows as
well as I do /   That the branch will not break. "   LJ

JAMES WRIGHT, WILLIAM DUFFY, ROBERT BLY

The Lion's Tail and Eyes.   The Sixties Press, 1962, 45 pages.

      This small introductory volume helps to fulfill one
purpose of The Sixties Press: to publish poets of the new
generation "whose work is moving in a direction different from
the direction of the old poetry. "   Through and around The
Sixties, the three poets represented here have emerged inde-
pendent of recent cults, with imaginative freshness, clear
voices, and concern both for communication and communion.
The subtitle, "Poems written out of laziness and silence, "
leads to Robert Bly's note: "A person meets the poem among
trees at night.   On the path in front of him, he sees a lion
who does not know that he is there. . . .   So far the tip of the
tail, the ears, the eyes, and perhaps a paw or two have
come. "   Those eyes flash in James Wright's "From a Bus
Window in Central Ohio. . . "; a paw or two shows in William
Duffy's "The Horse Is Loose"; and the whole presence is felt
in Bly's "Snowfall in the Afternoon. "   LJ

ALEKSANDR YESENIN-VOLPIN

A Leaf of Spring. Praeger, 1961, 175 pages.

        Poems of dissent in a bilingual edition and an an-
archist essay, written by the son of Sergey Yesenin, who
founded apolitical "Imaginist" (Russian Imagist) poetry and
committed suicide in 1925. The author was arrested first in
1948 and then placed in a psychiatric prison for his poems
including "The Raven," adapted from Poe, with its refrain:
"There's no rising ... nevermore!" There are poems of
savage bitterness in which all Muscovites are called "brutes,"
others of determined personal affirmation: "And one goal
alone is crystal clear, / The irrational goal of liberty!" The
title poem cries, "Pain is the only beauty that I know. "
Poetic revolt against Socialist Realism has its prose counter-
part in the second half of the book, "A Free Philosophical
Treatise" (dated July 1959), which attacks Marxist dogmas
as "pseudo-problems" of philosophy. Freedom is not "real-
ized necessity" (a slavemaster's definition) but "to choose
without compulsion" though the choice may not be pleasant.
The editor finds here a skepticism and nihilism far more de-
vastating than the "simple emptiness" of Western existential-
ism. Of his treatise, hastily prepared with hope for its
printing abroad, Yesenin-Volpin wrote: "There is no freedom
of the press in Russia, but who can say there is no freedom
of thought?"   LJ

ANDREW YOUNG

Quiet as Moss; Thirty-Six Poems. Dufour Editions, 1963,
40 pages.

A quiet, beautiful selection from Andrew Young presents 36 poems chosen by Leonard Clark, written in the clear tradition of English nature lyricism. Young has something of Housman's purity and ("A Child's Voice") Wordsworth's simplicity, almost accent. The aphoristic musing in "The Bird" brings Frost to mind: "I have enough to do/ In my own way to be unnoticed too. " In forthrightness, in sudden perspectives over countrysides and across time ("Wiltshire Downs"), he has closest affinity with Hardy (see too "The Track" and "In Teesdale"). Yet he is an original poet bringing his magic note to "sheep and shed and lighted rain. " Memorable poetry of nature and the heart of man, with its vivid compression well illustrated by Joan Hassall's wood-engravings.   LJ

RELATED ARTICLES BY RAY SMITH

A Brief Bibliography

"Book Selection and the Community Library, " in Carnovsky
and Winger, The Medium-Sized Public Library: Its
Status and Future, University of Chicago Press, 1963,
79-90. Also Library Quarterly, 33: 79-90 (Jan. 1963).

"Book Selection and the Imagination, " Minnesota Libraries,
22: 37-9 (Summer 1967).

"Legislators or Homogenizers, " Library Journal, 87:500-3
(Feb. 1, 1962).

"Manuscript Found in a Bottle: Gulliver Dui, " Wilson Library Bulletin, 38:401-3 (January 1964).

"The Outriders of the Great Community, " North Country
Anvil, No. 6:18-23 (June-July 1973).

APPENDIX

POETRY, SELECTION AND THE IMAGINATION

The greater part of book selection appears to be made within the orbit of library reviewing, so that, if it is to be improved, we librarians must raise our sights and ourselves together. As technical processes are lifted from many shoulders our main usefulness to our communities will stand out clearly: to mediate between them and the tide of books (nearly 40,000 titles published in the United States alone in 1973).

More and more, we need to think of selection and interpretation as two sides of one essential library process. Interpretation of books through newspaper annotations, talks, reviews in library literature in specialty fields--any and all help us to become what librarians ought to be first of all, active legislators in the republic of books.

We are charged by the nature of our position with a continual concern for books as more than counters in a game of circulation.

Alongside stress on the involvement of selection with interpretation I'd place the primacy of imagination for the

Adapted from an article in Minnesota Libraries (bibliography) by permission; presented at the Minnesota Library Division Waseca Workshop, Southern School of Agriculture in Waseca, Minnesota, April 1967.

public library. Surrounded and inundated by information--
"instant information, " epidermis deep--somebody in the community increasingly will need to "humanize the technology. "
We are the natural candidates.

Meridel Le Sueur, author of North Star Country, a
Knopf "wilderness road" series for young people, and most
recently Corn Village, has lived among Indians from Chippewa
to Pueblo in order to understand something of the traditions
which remain to them, and relate them to the Anglo traditions.
She asks in a letter: "Will the community live?" This is
the true question to which the selection of books and other library materials is related--not the new-modelism in books of
General Motors or Ford.

The community will live if its imaginative enactments
are relevant.

The library can prize and sustain a sense of continuity with the past, and quicken the community's awareness of
it as part of the continuing present. I think for our Indian
past of celebrating such a book as Black Elk Speaks, "the life
story of a Holy Man of the Oglala Sioux as told through John
G. Neihardt" (now in print as a paperbound by the University
of Nebraska Press).

We in the Middle West are only a long lifetime from
the frontier. As librarians and book people we can do much
in getting our indigenous literature born and walking by itself.
We can stimulate and make available new voices not in hard-
bound print.

On the primacy of the imagination and on its predic-
ament today, I quote a few sentences from the scientist (and
poet) Loren Eiseley's article "The Illusion of the Two Cul-
tures" (The American Scholar, Summer 1964):

> Our lives are the creation of memory and the
> accompanying power to extend ourselves outward
> into ideas and relive them.... (But:) Unconsci-
> ously the human realm is denied in favor of the
> world of pure technics. Man, the tool-user,
> grows convinced that he is himself useful only as
> a tool. We do not like mists in this era, and the
> word imagination is less and less used.... (Yet:)
> Man is not totally compounded of the nature we
> profess to understand. He contains, instead, a
> lurking unknown future.

"A lurking unknown future" leads to another emphasis
for me: our need for utopian (or dystopian) books, books
which contain imaginative, directive images of our possible
future. Henry Adams' Theory of Phase was in one sense be-
trayed by time, but so in one sense is life itself. Synthesis
is always more difficult than analysis but we need synthesis
in theoretical speculation and in creative vision. I am fond
myself of powerful directional books such as Teilhard de
Chardin's The Phenomenon of Man. (Probably the most remarkable book of our days, and not theology--is it often really
read?) Or, far more modest but worthwhile in its revelation
of the arbitrariness of accepted ways, Sedge by Louis J. Halle
("the anthropologico-psychologico-socio-politico-cultural complex of this remote and little-known country"):

> In Sedge, according to Pluvius, thinking occupies
> the place accorded to research in our society.
> "You, " he said, "start with research, and it some-
> times leads to thought. We start with thought and
> it sometimes leads to research. "

Poetry is the most imaginative and permanent means
of human communication and communion. As such, and because of all the arts it remains most remote from the general
public, it deserves library emphasis. Consider Max Frisch's
definition, which I like to quote: "Technology ... the knack
of so arranging the world that we don't have to experience it."

Whereas the meaning of poetry is in the experiencing. What
Vietnams we might avoid if we experienced the world, and
what dropping of the atom bomb "because we had it. "

    Verse is rhymed language with a patterned beat, a
possible vehicle for poetry which too often resembles it about
as much as a toy dog resembles a panther.   Too much ac-
cessible verse deals a body blow to poetry by being justly
identified as a sentimental decoration, a frosting on ordinary
speech, rather than an essential distillation of our language.

    The permanence and validity of poetic speech has
always been linked to a dual concern: with the inward of experience, and with the living language.   Wordsworth in
"Michael" aimed to, and did, lift common experience and
speech into poetry.   Not all poets and times have been able
to do this but it has remained the central stream to which
poetry has returned: Yeats in our century, or William Carlos
Williams experimenting with his "relative measure, " culminating in the wonderful love poem of his old age, "Asphodel,
That Greeny Flower. "

    It can be said of language and true poetry, as Elie
Faure said of experience and art, that they have the sameness
in kind but the difference in density of dust and granite.

    It would be suggestive to close with the unfinished
business given in Walt Whitman's pronouncement:

    One's-self I sing, a simple, separate person,
      Yet utter the word Democratic, the word En-Masse.
"The two are contradictory, " Whitman told his friend Horace
Traubel, "but our task is to reconcile them. "   The reconciliation of desirable individualism with desirable socialization is
our problem and our necessity.   In this task poetry and the
imagination are deeply, feelingly, and therefore effectively,
concerned.

INDEX

(Poets, Authors, Titles)

Index   137